1st EDITION

Perspectives on Modern World History

The Iranian Revolution

1st EDITION

Perspectives on Modern World History

The Iranian Revolution

Noah Berlatsky

Editor

GREENHAVEN PRESS

A part of Gale, Cengage Learning

GALE
CENGAGE Learning·

Detroit • New York • San Francisco • New Haven, Conn • Waterville, Maine • London

GALE
CENGAGE Learning·

Elizabeth Des Chenes, *Managing Editor*

© 2012 Greenhaven Press, a part of Gale, Cengage Learning.

Gale and Greenhaven Press are registered trademarks used herein under license.

For more information, contact:
Greenhaven Press
27500 Drake Rd.
Farmington Hills, MI 48331-3535
Or you can visit our Internet site at gale.cengage.com.

For product information and technology assistance, contact us at
Gale Customer Support, 1-800-877-4253.

For permission to use material from this text or product, submit all requests online at
www.cengage.com/permissions.

Further permissions questions can be e-mailed to permissionrequest@cengage.com.

Articles in Greenhaven Press anthologies are often edited for length to meet page requirements. In addition, original titles of these works are changed to clearly present the main thesis and to explicitly indicate the author's opinion. Every effort is made to ensure that Greenhaven Press accurately reflects the original intent of the authors. Every effort has been made to trace the owners of copyrighted material.

Cover images © Art Directors & TRIP/Alamy and © Mohammad Berno/Document Iran/Corbis.

LIBRARY OF CONGRESS CATALOGING-IN-PUBLICATION DATA
The Iranian Revolution / Noah Berlatsky, book editor.
   p. cm. -- (Perspectives on modern world history)
   Includes bibliographical references and index.
   ISBN 978-0-7377-5793-4 (hardcover)
   1. Iran--History--Revolution, 1979. 2. Iran--History--Revolution, 1979--Personal narratives. I. Berlatsky, Noah.
   DS318.81.I73 2012
   955.05'3--dc23
                                                        2011042696

Printed in the United States of America
1 2 3 4 5 6 7 16 15 14 13 12

CONTENTS

Foreword   1

Introduction   4

World Map   8

CHAPTER 1   Historical Background on the
                 Iranian Revolution

1. An Overview of the Iranian Revolution   11
   Eric Hooglund

   An encyclopedia article describes the mass,
   nationwide Iranian uprising of 1978–1979.
   The revolution ousted the ruling monarch, the
   shah, and replaced him with a fundamentalist
   Islamic government headed by the Ayatollah
   Khomeini.

2. The Shah Is Forced to Leave Iran   17
   Jonathan C. Randal

   An American newspaper article describes the
   circumstances of the shah's departure and the
   scenes of joy in Iran that followed.

3. Ayatollah Khomeini Proclaims an
   Islamic Republic   25
   Montreal Gazette

   A Canadian newspaper describes reaction
   to the national Iranian vote that ushered in
   an Islamic republic headed by the Ayatollah
   Khomeini.

4. The British Parliament Responds to
an Attack on Its Embassy in Iran   **29**

House of Commons Debate

Members of the British House of Commons
describe an attack on the British embassy in
Tehran. They insist that Iran must protect foreign diplomats, and discuss the implications
of the Iranian Revolution for British embassy
staff, for Iranians living in Britain, and for
British oil supplies.

5. The United States Fails to Free
Its Hostages in Iran   **38**

Robert Shaplen

An American magazine article discusses the
unsuccessful efforts by the US government to
free American hostages taken by Iran in the
period following the Iranian Revolution.

6. The Islamic Government in Iran
Restricts Women's Rights   **50**

Leslie Keith

An American newspaper article describes
growing restrictions on Iranian women a year
and a half after the revolution established an
Islamic government.

CHAPTER 2

Controversies Surrounding the Iranian Revolution

1. The United States Should Have
Supported the Shah More Fully   **56**

James Perloff

An American writer argues that the shah was
a just ruler and staunch US ally. He argues
that the United States' failure to support the

shah during the Iranian Revolution was a
moral and strategic disaster.

2. The United States Should Not Have Supported
   the Shah   **69**

   Anonymous

   Iranian Harvard students writing several
   months after the revolution argue that the
   shah was an unjust and cruel leader. They
   assert that the United States should not provide asylum for the shah.

3. The Western Press Unfairly Demonized
   the Iranian Revolution   **74**

   Edward W. Said

   A Palestinian American and leading intellectual argues in the year after the revolution
   that the American press unfairly portrayed
   events in Iran as unmotivated and irrational.
   He suggests that the representation was based
   on Western prejudices and American self-
   interest.

4. The Western Press Was Correct About
   the Dangers of the Iranian Revolution   **88**

   David Zarnett

   A British writer argues that the Western
   media's hostility to Khomeini was based on
   mounting evidence of the repressive and cruel
   nature of the Iranian theocracy.

5. The Islamic Revolution Promised
   Political Spirituality for All   **98**

   Michel Foucault

   A leading French intellectual argues in the
   months leading up to the Iranian Revolution
   that an Islamic government will allow for

more spiritual politics, which will benefit all Iranians.

6. The Islamic Revolution
   Betrayed Women   **110**

   Donna M. Hughes

   An American women's studies professor
   argues that women were active participants
   in the Iranian Revolution. They hoped to
   achieve greater freedom in a new Iran than
   under the shah's oppressive regime. Instead,
   the governments of the Ayatollah Khomeini
   and subsequent leaders have curtailed wom-
   en's rights.

7. The Iranian Green Revolution Has
   Dangerous Similarities to 1979   **122**

   Michael Singh

   A Middle East policy specialist argues that the
   Iranian Green Revolution of 2009–2010 has
   many parallels with the revolution of 1979.
   He concludes that the Green Revolution may
   eventually be successful, but it may result in
   instability, violence, and oppression as did the
   earlier revolution.

8. The Iranian Green Revolution Is Not
   Similar to 1979   **129**

   Danny Postel

   The communications coordinator of an interfaith labor organization argues that the Green
   Revolution is ideologically different from the
   1979 revolution in Iran. He concludes that
   the Green Revolution has real emancipating
   potential and deserves support.

CHAPTER 3 Personal Narratives

1. A British Diplomat's Eyewitness
   Account of the Revolution   137

   Desmond Harney

   The diary entries of a British diplomat stationed in Iran focus on his impressions of Iran
   and Khomeini in the days before and after the
   shah's exile.

2. An Iranian Professor Describes Her
   Ordeal During the Revolution   145

   Sattareh Farman Farmaian with Dona Munker

   A professor and social activist describes her
   arrest and near execution during the Iranian
   Revolution.

3. The Ayatollah Khomeini Discusses His
   Vision of Iran   157

   Ayatollah Khomeini, interviewed by Oriana Fallaci

   In an interview, the Ayatollah Khomeini discusses the crimes of the shah, political freedom, executions, and morality as they relate
   to the new regime in Iran.

4. Americans Captured in Iran Discuss
   Their Experiences as Hostages   165

   *Rocky Sickmann and William Gallegos, interviewed
   by Rita Cosby*

   Twenty-five years after their release from Iran,
   two American hostages discuss their capture,
   their ordeal in captivity, and their release.

5. Iranian Exiles Discuss Life After
   Leaving Iran   172

   *Mehrdad Haghighi and Lily, interviewed by
   Zohreh T. Sullivan*

Two Iranian exiles discuss fleeing from Iran and their experiences trying to make a new life for themselves in the United States.

Glossary   **178**

Chronology   **180**

For Further Reading   **182**

Index   **185**

FOREWORD

"History cannot give us a program for the future, but it can give us a fuller understanding of ourselves, and of our common humanity, so that we can better face the future."

—Robert Penn Warren,
American poet and novelist

The history of each nation is punctuated by momentous events that represent turning points for that nation, with an impact felt far beyond its borders. These events—displaying the full range of human capabilities, from violence, greed, and ignorance to heroism, courage, and strength—are nearly always complicated and multifaceted. Any student of history faces the challenge of grasping the many strands that constitute such world-changing events as wars, social movements, and environmental disasters. But understanding these significant historic events can be enhanced by exposure to a variety of perspectives, whether of people involved intimately or of ones observing from a distance of miles or years. Understanding can also be increased by learning about the controversies surrounding such events and exploring hot-button issues from multiple angles. Finally, true understanding of important historic events involves knowledge of the events' human impact—of the ways such events affected people in their everyday lives—all over the world.

Perspectives on Modern World History examines global historic events from the twentieth-century onward by presenting analysis and observation from numerous vantage points. Each volume offers high school, early college level, and general interest readers a thematically

1

arranged anthology of previously published materials that address a major historical event, with an emphasis on international coverage. Each volume opens with background information on the event, then presents the controversies surrounding that event, and concludes with first-person narratives from people who lived through the event or were affected by it. By providing primary sources from the time of the event, as well as relevant commentary surrounding the event, this series can be used to inform debate, help develop critical thinking skills, increase global awareness, and enhance an understanding of international perspectives on history.

Material in each volume is selected from a diverse range of sources, including journals, magazines, newspapers, nonfiction books, personal narratives, speeches, congressional testimony, government documents, pamphlets, organization newsletters, and position papers. Articles taken from these sources are carefully edited and introduced to provide context and background. Each volume of Perspectives on Modern World History includes an array of views on events of global significance. Much of the material comes from international sources and from US sources that provide extensive international coverage.

Each volume in the Perspectives on Modern World History series also includes:

- A full-color **world map**, offering context and geographic perspective.
- An annotated **table of contents** that provides a brief summary of each essay in the volume.
- An **introduction** specific to the volume topic.
- For each viewpoint, a brief **introduction** that has notes about the author and source of the viewpoint, and that provides a summary of its main points.
- Full-color **charts**, **graphs**, **maps**, and other visual representations.

- Informational **sidebars** that explore the lives of key individuals, give background on historical events, or explain scientific or technical concepts.
- A **glossary** that defines key terms, as needed.
- A **chronology** of important dates preceding, during, and immediately following the event.
- A **bibliography** of additional books, periodicals, and websites for further research.
- A comprehensive **subject index** that offers access to people, places, and events cited in the text.

Perspectives on Modern World History is designed for a broad spectrum of readers who want to learn more about not only history but also current events, political science, government, international relations, and sociology—students doing research for class assignments or debates, teachers and faculty seeking to supplement course materials, and others wanting to improve their understanding of history. Each volume of Perspectives on Modern World History is designed to illuminate a complicated event, to spark debate, and to show the human perspective behind the world's most significant happenings of recent decades.

INTRODUCTION

The leader of the Islamic Iranian Revolution, Ruhollah Khomeini, was born in 1902 in the poor rural town of Khumayn, Iran, to a family known for its religious learning. His father was murdered by bandits shortly after Khomeini was born; his mother died when he was fifteen years old.

Despite these personal tragedies, Khomeini showed himself adept in religious studies in Shia Islam, the main Muslim denomination in Iran. He learned first from his brother, and later attended classes with important Islamic scholars. He moved to the holy city of Qum to continue his work. He finished his theological studies by 1927, after which he became a qualified jurist, or *mujahid.*

Completing his studies, Khomeini became a teacher himself, specializing in Islamic philosophy and jurisprudence. His reputation as a scholar and religious thinker grew. He published his first important book, *Kashif al-Asrar* (*Secrets Revealed*), in 1942. The book advocated for greater control of government by the clergy. However, at this stage, "Khomeini's pronouncements were more or less in line with the apolitical and nonrevolutionary stance of the Shia clerical establishment," according to Mehdi Moslem in his 2002 book *Factional Politics in Post-Khomeini Iran.*

Khomeini's mentor, Ayatollah Hosayn Borujerdi, opposed open conflict with the government; as a result, Khomeini did not engage in politics through most of the 1950s. Nonetheless, his fame increased, and his speeches attracted thousands. Khomeini's first major political exposure occurred in 1962, following Borujerdi's death, when he denounced a liberal reform package put forward by the government of the Iranian monarch, Mohammad

Reza Shah Pahlavi. The government measures included votes for women and land reform, and they allowed the Baha'is, a religious minority, to be elected to office. The reform package also granted diplomatic immunity to US military personnel in Iran. Khomeini opposed all these provisions strongly. He also gained notoriety for his strong opposition to the shah's support of Israel. In a heated 1964 speech, quoted in Behrouz Souresrafil's 1989 book *Khomeini and Israel*, Khomeini declared, "the economy of this country is in the hands of Israel and its agents. . . . We have to cut the root of imperialism by cutting this relationship with Israel."

In this period Khomeini was arrested several times. One of his incarcerations sparked days of demonstrations that provoked a government crackdown that resulted in dozens of deaths. In 1964, Khomeini was exiled. He settled in Najaf, Iraq, where he further developed his ideas about government. In particular, he proposed the idea of *velayat-e faqeeh*, which called for government by the Islamic clergy. Khomeini continued to speak out against the shah and maintained contact with a network of supporters within Iran, who smuggled his sermons into the country on audiocassette.

In early 1978, the official media in Iran began a campaign to discredit Khomeini. Protests against the campaign erupted and continued for months, becoming a real threat to the shah's regime. Khomeini urged the demonstrations on, refusing calls for compromise. Under pressure from Iran, Iraq forced him out of the country, and he relocated to Paris. There he had greater access to the Western press, and he continued to encourage revolution. Having lost political control of his country, the shah fled Iran on January 16, 1979, and Khomeini "returned in triumph . . . to a delirious welcome from 3 million supporters who thronged the airport and streets of Tehran," according to Christopher M. Andrew and Vasili Mitrokhin in their 2005 book *The World Was*

Going Our Way: The KGB and the Battle for the Third World. In March 1979, the hereditary monarchy officially ended in Iran, and it became an Islamic republic with final authority placed on a religious leader. That leader was Khomeini for his lifetime.

There did remain moderates and secular leaders with power in Iran, but Khomeini was able to consolidate his position against them in large part through the hostage crisis of November 1979. At that time, Islamic students overran the US embassy in Tehran, the capital of Iran, and took sixty-six Americans hostage, demanding that the shah, who had fled to the United States, be returned to Iran for trial. The plight of the hostages caused a media firestorm in the United States and around the world. It also helped shape domestic politics in Iran. "Whereas the crisis was a boon for the radical mullahs, it was an absolute disaster for the secular and clerical moderates. Anti-Americanism became the test of one's loyalty to the revolution and the hostage crisis itself became a reflection of domestic political needs," according to Matthew RJ Brodsky on an article at the website Middle East Opinion. By the time the hostages were released in early 1981, Khomeini had successfully purged most liberal elements from power.

Even before the resolution of the hostage crisis, Khomeini had become embroiled in the major conflict of his rule in Iran: the Iran-Iraq war. The secular Iraqi dictator, Saddam Hussein, "felt directly threatened by the Islamic revolution, which had brought Ayatollah Khomeini to power in Iran," according to Roger Hardy in a September 22, 2005, article on the BBC website. Hussein worried that the religious Iranian regime would cause unrest in Iraq and ultimately topple his government. Therefore, in September 1980, Hussein used a dispute over a waterway as an excuse to invade Iran. He believed that he would be able to achieve a quick victory. Instead, the war dragged on for two years, by which time Iran had pushed Iraqi forces back to their own borders.

At this point, Iraq offered a cease-fire, but Khomeini refused. Instead, he attempted to push into Iraq. The two sides fought for another six years, resulting in deaths estimated at between half a million and 1.5 million people. Khomeini, faced with international opposition and exhaustion at home, finally agreed to end the conflict in July 1988. But his years of intransigence damaged revolutionary fervor in Iran and made many Iranians question the wisdom of clerical rule.

Khomeini died barely a year after the end of the Iran-Iraq war, on June 3, 1989, at the age of eighty-six. His death prompted a massive outpouring of grief. Three and a half million people attended his funeral, which had to be aborted when mourners tore apart the wooden coffin in order to get a final glimpse of the dead leader.

Despite the repressive nature of clerical rule, the tragedy of the Iran-Iraq war, and recent protests against the Islamic regime, Khomeini remains widely honored in Iran. A ceremony on the anniversary of his death at his shrine at the Behesht-e-Zahra cemetery draws hundreds of thousands of people every year.

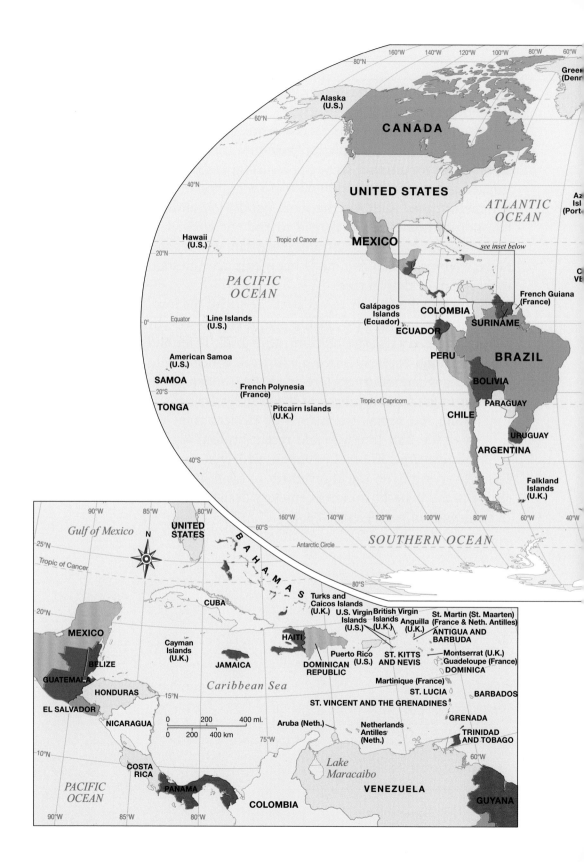

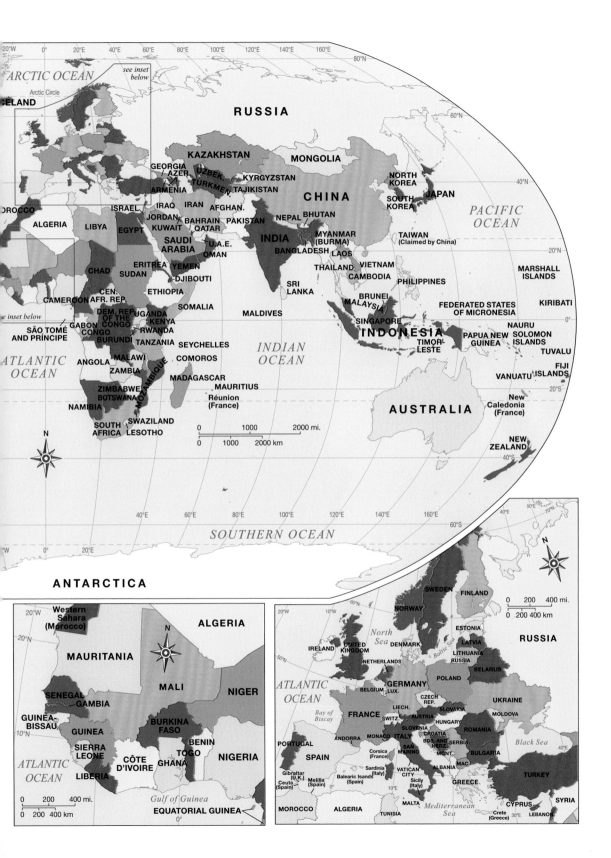

CHAPTER 1

Historical Background on the Iranian Revolution

An Overview of the Iranian Revolution

Eric Hooglund

The following viewpoint outlines the events of the Iranian Revolution. The author explains that during 1978 and 1979, the government of Mohammad Reza Shah Pahlavi (known as the shah, a Persian term meaning "king") was overthrown by a popular movement. The leader of the movement was Ayatollah Ruhollah Khomeini, a high-ranking Muslim clergyman living in exile in Iraq. Khomeini appealed to both secular and religious groups, and his message inspired massive protests throughout Iran. The shah attempted to repress these protests, but when the military killed civilians, the resistance merely became more heated. Eventually the shah was forced to leave the country. Khomeini returned to Iran and established a new government under his control. Eric Hooglund is a professor of politics at Bates College and editor of the journal *Middle East Critique*.

Photo on previous page: Ayatollah Ruhollah Khomeini waves to supporters in Tehran, Iran, shortly after his return, in February 1979, from fifteen years of exile. (**Gabriel Duval/ AFP/Getty Images.**)

In February 1979, the regime of Mohammad Reza Shah Pahlavi collapsed in the face of an organized popular revolution. This event marked the end of over 450 years of monarchical rule that had begun with the establishment of the Safavid dynasty in 1501; a republican form of government replaced the deposed monarchy. Some scholars trace the origins of the Iranian Revolution to the 1953 coup d'état against the prime minister and National Front leader Mohammad Mossadegh or to the abortive 1963 uprisings sparked by the arrest of Ayatollah Ruhollah Khomeini. The more immediate cause of the revolution, however, was the failure of the shah's government to address the multifaceted cultural, economic, political, and social grievances that had been building up in Iranian society during the 1970s. The shah not only ignored these grievances but used his secret police agency, the SAVAK, to repress expressions of discontent and both real and suspected opposition activities.

Khomeini Unites the Anti-Shah Movement

During 1978, Khomeini was the person who succeeded in uniting the diverse currents of discontent into a unified anti-shah movement. He was a senior clergyman of Shi'ism[1] living in exile in Iraq since 1965. Khomeini effectively used popular Shi'ite themes, such as the moral and religious righteousness of struggling against oppression and for justice, to appeal broadly to both religious and secular Iranians. By 1977, his network of former students had begun circulating tapes of his sermons at religious gatherings; these sermons denounced the shah's injustice and called for strict adherence to the 1906 constitution, which had established a constitutional monarchy, with the shah subordinate to the elected Majles, or parliament. (The shah, like his father before him, had asserted his authority over the Majles by controlling

The Roots of the Shah's Fall

The many diplomatic and economic achievements of the shah led to ostentatious displays of royal hubris. For example, in October 1971 he celebrated the 2,500th anniversary of the foundation of the Persian Empire by Cyrus the Great and formed, in March 1975, a one-party system. Both acts were resented by the intelligentsia and middle classes. He also replaced powerful, independent-minded politicians with more accommodating and submissive aides, a strategy that cost him dearly at times of international and domestic crisis. Concurrently, the shah's White Revolution [a series of social, political, and economic reforms begun in 1963] had undermined the traditional foundation of his authority—the *ulama*, the bazaar merchants, and the landowning classes. They were replaced by the entrepreneurs, the young Western-educated bureaucratic elites, and new middle classes who had developed uneasy relations with the shah. The intelligentsia resented the lack of political freedom and violations of human rights, the rigged elections, corruption, and close ties with the United States. The old religious groups and the bazaar merchants and artisans resented the un-Islamic Western lifestyle promoted by the shah's modernization policies. The entrepreneurial and political elites were discontented with the shah's autocratic rule, and with the lack of their own political power and autonomous organizational base. Under these circumstances the nucleus of an anti-shah revolutionary coalition was formed by a large group of liberal and radical intelligentsia, and a small group of militant *ulama* and their important followers in the bazaar.

SOURCE. *Ahmad Ashraf, "Pahlavi, Mohammad Reza [1919–1980],"* Encyclopedia of the Modern Middle East and North Africa, *2nd ed., vol. 3, ed. Philip Mattar. New York: Macmillan Reference USA, 2004, pp. 1752–1755.*

parliamentary elections and creating what in practice amounted to a royal dictatorship.) The government tried to counteract Khomeini's growing popularity by placing in a pro-regime newspaper an article that defamed the ayatollah's character. Its publication provoked major protest demonstrations in Qom (January 1978), which resulted in several deaths and the closure of the city's bazaars. The incident galvanized opposition to the shah and set in motion a cycle of protest demonstrations—and brutal repression—every forty days, the fortieth day after a death being a traditional Iranian commemoration of the deceased.

By August 1978, it had become obvious that the repressive tactics that had worked in the past no longer were effective in containing the ever-growing protest movement. The shah sought to defuse the opposition by appointing a new government of royalist politicians who had maintained ties to the clergy, by freeing some political prisoners, and by relaxing press censorship. This led to a major demonstration in Tehran, where more than 100,000 people marched through the city carrying photos of Khomeini and handing out flowers to the soldiers and police; the latter were asked to join the call for free elections. Similar peaceful but smaller-scale demonstrations took place in many other cities. Apparently frightened by the strength of the movement and the evident solidarity among religious and secular groups, the shah declared martial law in Tehran and eleven other cities and ordered the arrest of National Front and Freedom Movement leaders. The first day of martial law, 8 September 1978, became known as Black Friday because several hundred people were killed in Tehran as troops forced thousands of demonstrators to leave the area of the parliament building, where they had gathered to demand free elections.

> "The first day of martial law . . . became known as Black Friday because several hundred people were killed in Tehran.

The Growing Strength of the Revolution

Black Friday first stunned and then enraged the people. In response to urging from Khomeini, strikes spread throughout the country, affecting factories, shops,

Government and bank documents and burning cars and furniture cover a street in downtown Tehran following a day of demonstrations and looting November 4, 1978. (**Kaveh Kazemi/ Getty Images.**)

schools, the oil industry, utilities, and the press. By the end of October, Iran's economy was paralyzed. The shah appointed a military government with authority to force oil workers and others back to their jobs. He also freed imprisoned National Front, Freedom Movement, and clerical leaders in hopes that they would go to Paris, where Khomeini had moved, and convince the ayatollah to moderate his views. These tactics failed. Many army conscripts were refusing to shoot at unarmed civilians and even deserting their units, and the strikes continued. Khomeini announced he would accept nothing less than the removal of the shah, and the main secular and religious opposition leaders supported his position. Despite the military government, demonstrations continued throughout November, and each day produced more martyrs as people were killed in cities and towns when the army tried to suppress protest marches. It was clear that the shah's government had lost control of the streets. Fearful of more bloodshed

> Khomeini announced he would accept nothing less than the removal of the shah, and the main secular and religious opposition leaders supported his position.

during the Shi'ite religious month of Muharram (the religious calendar is a lunar one, and Muharram began on 1 December in 1978), the government agreed to allow traditional mourning processions if religious leaders promised to keep order. Millions of Iranians participated in peaceful marches throughout the country, but instead of mourning the martyrdom of the saint Imam Hosain, they called for the downfall of the shah. The popular slogan chanted everywhere became "*Azadi, Istiqlal, Jomhuri Islami*" (freedom, independence, Islamic republic). These terms meant political freedom from the oppression of the secret police, independence from the shah's alliance with the United States, and a republican government based on Islamic principles of justice.

The popular message of Muharram was clear, even to the shah, who now sought a dignified way to leave Iran and preserve the throne for his eighteen-year-old son. He persuaded longtime National Front opponent Shapur Bakhtiar to form a government. On 16 January 1979, the shah left Iran on a trip officially described as a medical rest. On 1 February 1979, Khomeini, triumphantly returned from exile, refused to recognize the legitimacy of Bakhtiar's government and appointed a provisional government headed by Freedom Movement leader Mehdi Bazargan. Demonstrations against Bakhtiar and in favor of Bazargan took place throughout the country. On 11 February 1979, military leaders ordered their forces back to their barracks and to remain neutral in the civilian political struggle. This announcement led to the collapse of the Bakhtiar government and the victory of the revolutionary movement.

Note

1. Shiism is a denomination of Islam. It is the majority denomination in Iran.

The Shah Is Forced to Leave Iran

Jonathan C. Randal

The following viewpoint describes the reaction in Tehran, the Iranian capital, following the departure of the ruling shah in January 1979. The author says that people danced in the street and celebrated the downfall of the hated leader. Foreigners in Tehran, however, were cautious, he says, fearing that popular anger would be directed at them. Iranians were also anticipating the return of Ayatollah Khomeini, the exiled leader of the revolution. Some feared that there would be continued conflict, while others hoped that Iran would establish a free and democratic government. Jonathan C. Randal is a former Middle East correspondent for the *Washington Post* and the author of *Osama: The Making of a Terrorist*.

Tehran [Iran's capital] erupted into wild scenes of joy today [January 16, 1979] once it became clear that Shah Mohammad Reza Pahlavi had indeed left the country.

Dancing in the Streets

Girls tossed flowers from upper floors. Civilians embraced soldiers and put carnations in their gun barrels. Statues of the shah and his father were torn down.

People danced in the streets. Motorists honked horns, turned on headlights, even set their windshield wipers in motion as signs of joy, while passengers leaned out doors, screamed their happiness and flashed the V for victory sign.

> People danced in the streets. Motorists honked horns, turned on headlights, even set their windshield wipers in motion as signs of joy.

The uncertainties that lie ahead for this nation in revolutionary midstream were clearly visible. But such have been the tensions of the year-long struggle to oust the shah that Iranians appear determined to savor what could turn out to be one of their last days of such broad unity.

A long-repressed people, Iranians did their best today to appear a smiling, laughing and good-natured lot—even with Americans, whose country is being blamed for Iran's ills now that the shah has gone.

"Shah gone," announced enormous 120-point type headlines in the evening newspaper *Ettalaat*. Its front page featured a photograph of the shah waving farewell as he was about to enter the airliner he flew to Egypt.

The now familiar "death to the shah" chanted by crowds throughout the long struggle began to give way today to "after the shah, now the Americans."

A freshly painted sign said, "Yankees go home now, the shah is dead."

Foreign correspondents reported receiving anonymous telephone calls announcing, "The shah is gone: now you leave." But Iranians were friendly when they met Americans in Tehran.

"I'm sorry for the people of your country," a young man said, after castigating only recently reversed American government support for the shah, "because the shah is going to your country and he'll make things dirty for you."

A cartoon displayed by passengers in a honking car showed President [Jimmy] Carter standing next to a shah whose neck was in a noose. The caption said: "Bye, bye."

Other signs of disrespect of the much-hated but once-feared monarch included drawings showing him dressed as a jailbird or a sexy woman, or in a uniform festooned variously with the Nazi swastika, the letters U.S.A. and the Star of David.

The United States and Israel, close allies of the shah, long have been singled out as enemies of the revolution led by the Moslem clergy.

The day's favorite trick was cutting the shah's bust out of banknotes. Most of the banknotes thus sacrificed were of small denominations, but at least one man thought nothing of cutting up a 1,000-rial note, worth $14.

Foreigners Exhibit Caution

Word of the royal couple's departure was broadcast on the 2 P.M. radio news, more than half an hour after the airplane had taken off. It caught many Iranians at the lunch table, but within minutes of the broadcast the first car horns were blaring in a pattern that went on well into the night.

With the shah gone, prudence became the order of the day for foreigners. At the Intercontinental Hotel, a 31 percent government-owned establishment favored by the foreign press, the management turned large lobby paintings of the shah and the empress to the wall.

> 'We wanted to hang [the shah] for all the evil he has done.'

By way of contrast, booksellers near Tehran University displayed Marxist literature that only recently has been sold openly, and also the banned novel "Crash of '79" in Persian, which has been on sale for only the past two days.

The title was accurate enough, even if the novel presents the shah as a power-mad maniac who destroys himself and his regime in nuclear war with Saudi Arabia.

About a half-mile away, Iranians clambered up two floors to remove and drop to the street below a commercial neon sign of a crown. One of the many groups of demonstrators in the capital's streets clearly was disappointed that the shah had been allowed to escape.

"We wanted to hang him for all the evil he has done," a young man said.

Elsewhere, a dog wandered with the following sign on his back: "Fellow countrymen, my traitor brother has just escaped. Please arrest and punish him."

At Tehran University, which has become the focal point for all shades of opposition thinking since Prime Minister Shahpour Bakhtiar[1] ordered troops away from the campus last week, a young lawyer said: "The departure announcement said he was going on vacation. Let me correct that. He has left forever, and we will never let him back, even if we have to fight to the death."

A few yards away, a happy crowd carried a turbaned mullah, a Moslem clergyman, on their shoulders before listening to him preach.

"Tonight we are going to have a big party with dancing and laughing and drinking—yes, even beer—to celebrate," a bearded young man said. "SAVAK (the secret police) and the CIA are finished, and I am 100 percent happy."

Were any reason needed to explain why Iranians so deeply hate SAVAK and the CIA, which helped set up its

Iranian counterpart in the late 1950s, they were supplied by a man in his 30s. He took off his right shoe and sock and, holding his naked right foot in his hand, displayed a large scar on the instep which he said was the result of SAVAK torture.

On January 16, 1979, Mohammad Reza Shah Pahlavi and Empress Farah left Iran, ending 450 years of monarchical rule. **(AP Photo.)**

An Uncertain Future

If Iranians seemed united in their condemnation of the past, no such unanimity existed about their views of the future. A foreign journalist listening to a man talk about politics had his sleeve plucked by a third person who said, "Don't listen to him. Don't write a thing. He is a communist."

Time and again Iranians insisted. "We are Moslems—not communists." This is to disprove the shah's propa-

The Shah Leaves

On January 16 [1979] the Shah's departure triggered an absolute carnival of rejoicing in the streets of Tehran. In the few minutes which elapsed after the radio broadcast the news, just about the whole population of the capital thronged into the streets, to cries of "*Shah raft!*" (The Shah has gone). People embraced one another. Cars honked their horns. The scale of the response and the spontaneity of an entire nation's rejoicing impressed every outside observer. The crowd fraternized with the soldiers, while demonstrators pulled down the statues of the sovereign and his father. Slogans rang out on all sides: "Our party is Allah's party, and our leader is Khomeini"; "The final victory is the Islamic Republic"; "After the Shah, it's Bakhtiar's turn."

At the airport the haggard Shah told [new prime minister Shahpur] Bakhtiar, "Your government has my complete confidence and I hope that its members' patriotism will enable each of them to bring their difficult tasks to a successful conclusion."

ganda saying all the opposition is made up of what he called "Islamic Marxists."

Nor could Iranians agree whether the Bakhtiar government should be given a chance or rather swept away as Ayatollah Ruhollah Khomeini, the Paris-based Moslem opposition leader, would seem to favor.

"Bakhtiar is dead," a student said.

But a young engineering graduate argued. "His is a medium good government," as if to suggest the prime minister should be given at least a chance to get the country back to work after months of turmoil.

Another point of discord is between Khomeini partisans, who want to abolish the monarchy and establish an Islamic government, and the more lay-minded Iranians who want a more Western-style republic.

Many are wondering when Khomeini will return to Iran. Some people were convinced it would be Friday to

The task in question was the restoration of order and the salvation of the monarchy. Bakhtiar had the Army to take care of order. To save the monarchy he was ready to sacrifice to the people those whom the Shah had singled out and jailed. . . . If they condemned to death a former Prime Minister, a former head of SAVAK [the secret police] and a batch of ministers and officials, the Shah would be cleansed of his sins, and then he could return. That is why the sovereign told those officers in the Imperial Guard who threw themselves on their knees and begged him to remain, "Don't worry, I won't be away for long." Yet again he was deceiving himself. The Shah's supporters and the moneyed classes did not fall for these fine words. They knew that a chapter was ending, and they packed their bags and quietly followed the Shah's example.

SOURCE. *Fereydoun Hoveyda,* The Fall of the Shah, *trans. Roger Liddell. New York: Wyndham Books, 1980, pp. 200–201.*

lead a day of demonstrations which he has asked to be the biggest in a year already full of huge marches.

Others said they simply did not know when he would come.

A key factor in determining his return was spotlighted by an army lieutenant named Mohammed Bashir, a recent University of Illinois engineering graduate who is teaching English at a military school.

Dressed in civilian clothes, he confirmed reports that Khomeini's recent orders to move the army over

> Not all Iranians were pleased with the shah's departure.

to his side seemed to be working. If that indeed were the case, perhaps Iranians were justified in their faith in Khomeini's ability to curb the armed forces, the last bastion of resistance to his march to power.

Not all Iranians were pleased with the shah's departure. Those chagrined varied from weeping women in government offices to hotel chambermaids fearful of the future without the shah, who for so long has symbolized unquestioned authority.

Abdel Karim Lahidji, a leading lawyer in the anti-shah opposition and a founding member of the Human Rights Committee, said, "When I finally heard the news on the radio, I said to myself that after 25 years of dictatorship, what a chance for democracy and freedom.

"I'm waiting for tomorrow," he said, "when the real struggle starts for democracy—tolerance for ourselves, prevention of anarchy, the start of a democratic life under the rule of law."

Note

1. Shapour (also spelled Shahpur) Bakhtiar was installed as prime minister before the shah left the country.

Ayatollah Khomeini Proclaims an Islamic Republic

Montreal Gazette

In the following viewpoint, a Canadian newspaper reports on the Iranian referendum in March-April 1979 on the establishment of an Iranian republic under the rule of the Ayatollah Ruhollah Khomeini. The paper says that the referendum was very popular, but suggests that, despite statements by Khomeini, it did not receive 100 percent of the vote. The article also notes that the central Iranian government faced unrest in some provinces where the Persian, Shiite Muslim central government is not popular.

Ayatollah Ruhollah Khomeini triumphantly proclaimed Iran an Islamic republic yesterday, saying almost all Iranians had voted for creation of the country's first "government of God."

SOURCE. "Khomeini Proclaims a 'Government of God,'" Associated Press, April 2, 1979. Used by permission.

> [Khomeini's] countrymen had voted 'to establish a government of righteousness and to overthrow and bury the monarchy in the garbage can of history.'

The 78-year-old Shiite Moslem leader, who led the struggle that toppled Shah Mohammad Reza Pahlavi in mid-February, said his countrymen had voted "to establish a government of righteousness and to overthrow and bury the monarchy in the garbage can of history."

Khomeini's statement, read by an announcer over Tehran radio, contrasted with continued concern by the revolutionary government over unrest among Iran's large ethnic minority groups.

Prime Minister Mehdi Bazargan, head of the Khomeini appointed provisional government, warned rebellious Turkoman tribesmen in the northeastern city of Gon-bad-e-Qabous yesterday that if the bloody week-old fighting there did not cease he would send in government troops Tuesday to restore order. At least 50 people have been killed and hundreds wounded. A government official warned, meanwhile, that new trouble was brewing in Arab-populated and oil-rich Khuzestan province. Besides renewing long-standing demands for greater political autonomy from the central government, which is dominated by Persians who comprise 50 per cent of Iran's 34 million people, many ethnic minorities, largely Sunni Moslems, resent domination by Khomeini's Shiite sect.

Khomeini said the country-wide referendum Friday and Saturday gave unanimous approval to an Islamic republic. But this apparently was not meant literally, since early returns on the weekend indicated a small number of Iranians voted against establishing an Islamic republic, which has still not been fully defined.

State radio and television said yesterday that preliminary results showed 18 million voted for the Islamic republic. An estimated 18.7 million people had been

More than a million people gathered at a rally around the Shah Memorial (later Freedom Tower) on January 19, 1979, to show their support for an Islamic republic in Iran. (**AP Photo/Bob Dear.**)

eligible to vote. As the results were announced, some motorists in downtown Tehran flashed their headlights to show approval. But most citizens seemed to take the news as a foregone conclusion.

> 'This is what the people had a revolution for.'

A Tehran bazaar merchant said: "Of course I expected it because it was obvious. This is what the people had a revolution for."

Khomeini sought to overthrow the shah because, among other reasons, his Western-style modernization of Iran ran counter to traditional Islamic values.

But at one voting booth in a middle-class section of Tehran, support for the republic ran at only about 70 per cent, said officials.

The British Parliament Responds to an Attack on Its Embassy in Iran

House of Commons Debate

The House of Commons is a legislative body of Great Britain. In the following viewpoint, House members discuss an attack on the British embassy in Tehran, Iran, in November 1979. The main speaker is Douglas Hurd, the minister of state in charge of foreign affairs. The House members insist that Iran must protect foreign diplomats, and they discuss the possibility of sanctions if the government fails to do so. They also discuss the importance of coordinating with the United States to deal with possible interruptions in oil supplies. Finally, they discuss the implications of the Iranian Revolution for British embassy staff and embassy families, and for Iranians living in Britain who may face political reprisals if they return home.

SOURCE. "House of Commons Debate," *Hansard*, v. 973, no. cc225-8, November 6, 1979.

Mr. Eldon Griffiths (by private notice) asked the Lord Privy Seal if he will make a statement about the attack on the British embassy in Tehran [Iran's capital].

Safety and Oil Supply

The Minister of State, Foreign and Commonwealth Office (Mr. Douglas Hurd): At about 10 minutes to six yesterday evening, Tehran time, armed intruders broke into the British embassy compound and shortly thereafter took over the whole of our embassy building. The staff in the area at the time were taken, together with those wives and children who live in the embassy compound, to the house of the chargé d'affaires, Mr. [Arthur] Wyatt. They were not ill-treated, but were held under armed guard. The identity of the intruders and the motives for their attack on the embassy are still not wholly clear. Contacts between embassy officials and the intruders took place over a period of about five hours, after which they withdrew from the premises.

We have protested strongly to the Iranian Government at this attack on our embassy. A protest was made to the Ministry of Foreign Affairs in Tehran and I spoke yesterday afternoon to the counsellor in charge of the Iranian embassy here. It is imperative that the Iranian Government fulfil their clear obligations under the Vienna convention and take adequate measures to protect diplomatic lives and premises.

Mr. Griffiths: I am grateful to my hon[orable] Friend. Will he please answer the following questions? What is the position of other British nationals in Iran? How many are there, and are they safe? What is to be the position about relations between Iran and any other Government, including our own, if diplomatic missions are not guaranteed to be inviolate?

Will my hon[orable] Friend give an undertaking that since there must be a likelihood that Iran will not,

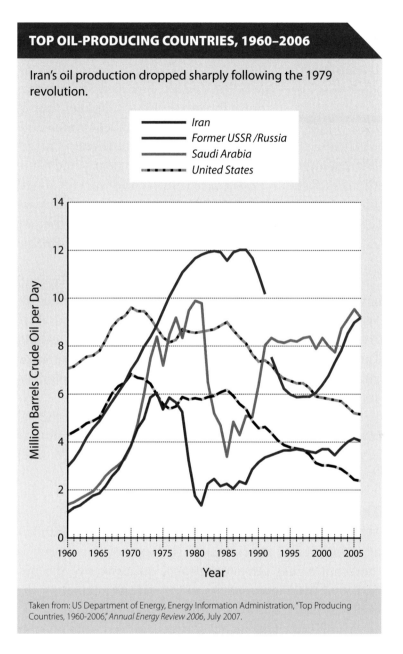

TOP OIL-PRODUCING COUNTRIES, 1960–2006

Iran's oil production dropped sharply following the 1979 revolution.

- Iran
- Former USSR /Russia
- Saudi Arabia
- United States

Million Barrels Crude Oil per Day

Year

Taken from: US Department of Energy, Energy Information Administration, "Top Producing Countries, 1960-2006," *Annual Energy Review 2006*, July 2007.

or will not be able to, deliver its supplies of oil, there are contingency plans available in Europe and with the Americans to avoid a further scramble of the sort that we saw last time? Will he also give an undertaking that the

Government will not be a party to arrangements to send back the Shah, a sick man, to meet the blood lust of the Tehran mob?

Mr. Hurd: The British community in Iran, although smaller than it used to be, still numbers about 500. It is not under direct threat. The attack on the embassy clearly had some political intention and was not aimed at individuals, but one reason why we are determined to keep an embassy in Iran is that there is still a sizeable British community there.

> Our embassies and those of other countries are increasingly at risk. Two of our ambassadors have been murdered in the past few years.

We were in touch yesterday and have been in touch again today with our Community partners and the United States on my hon[orable] Friend's second point. If there be a Government, calling themselves a Government, in Tehran, one of their clear duties under international law is to protect the diplomats accredited to them.

Of course, we are all the time considering the oil supply situation and what action we and our friends may have to take. I entirely agree with what my hon[orable] Friend said about the Shah.

The Vienna Convention

Mr. [Thomas] Dalyell: Given the increasing vulnerability of embassies of all countries throughout the world, is there not a case for international discussion of the updating of the Vienna convention [a treaty regulating the international law of treaties between countries]?

Mr. Hurd: That is very much in our minds. Our embassies and those of other countries are increasingly at risk. Two of our ambassadors have been murdered in the past few years. But however hard one considers the matter one is driven back to the conclusion that although we can secure embassies against an individual intruder,

Iran Reclaims Its Oil Fields from Great Britain

Since the early years of the twentieth century a British company, owned mainly by the British government, had enjoyed a fantastically lucrative monopoly on the production and sale of Iranian oil. The wealth that flowed from beneath Iran's soil played a decisive role in maintaining Britain at the pinnacle of world power while most Iranians lived in poverty. Iranians chafed bitterly under this injustice. Finally, in 1951, they turned to [Mohammad] Mossadegh [also spelled Mussaddaq], who more than any other political leader personified their anger at the Anglo-Iranian Oil Company (AIOC). He pledged to throw the company out of Iran, reclaim the country's vast petroleum reserves, and free Iran from subjection to foreign power.

Prime Minister Mossadegh carried out his pledges with single-minded zeal. To the ecstatic cheers of his people, he nationalized Anglo-Iranian, the most profitable British business in the world. Soon afterward, Iranians took control of the company's giant refinery at Abadan on the Persian Gulf.

This sent Iran into patriotic ecstasy and made Mossadegh a national hero. It also outraged the British, who indignantly accused Mossadegh of stealing their property. They first demanded that the World Court and the United Nations punish him, then sent warships to the Persian Gulf, and finally imposed a crushing embargo that devastated Iran's economy.

SOURCE. *Stephen Kinzer,* All the Shah's Men: An American Coup and the Roots of Middle East Terror. *Hoboken, NJ: John Wiley & Sons, 2003, pp. 2–3.*

The Union Jack is seen through one of the many shattered windows of Iran's British embassy, which was heavily damaged by mob violence in November 1978. (AP Photo/D. Ive.)

there is no escaping the fact that when an armed mob appears the responsibility for protecting an embassy must rest on the host Government. However we look at the problem, that is the answer that we are forced back to.

Mr. [Peter] Temple-Morris: Is my hon[orable] Friend aware that we are perhaps not at the end of the road of Tehran-based emergencies? Does he agree that yesterday's events and any future events must have a cool and firm response from the Government? As part of that response, will the Government make clear on any occasion that demands it that the Iranian Government and people cannot eat without the West, and the help of the West, and that there is nowhere else for them, with their theocracy, to go?

Mr. Hurd: I agree with my hon[orable] Friend. I do not think that we can let the matter of yesterday's incident—which, as far as we are concerned, is closed—rest there. That is why we are in touch with the other Community countries represented in Tehran and with the United

States. Further action will be required to bring home to the authorities in Tehran that under international law they have a clear obligation, which they have been neglecting.

Mr. [Peter] Shore: We strongly endorse and reinforce the protest made by the Government, both in respect of the occupation of the British embassy and the temporary detention of British wives and children in Tehran.

Can the Minister say anything about reports that the [Mehdi] Bazargan Government [the first government after the revolution] have tendered their resignation? If there is to be a change of Government in Tehran, will the hon[orable] Gentleman make clear to whoever takes on responsibility that we expect minimum standards of conduct in relation to our diplomats, since otherwise it will not be worth having diplomacy in countries that so flagrantly flout the rules? Will the Minister also consult urgently other oil-consuming countries about arrangements that may have to be made if oil supplies from Iran are intercepted?

Mr. Hurd: I am grateful for what the right hon[orable] Gentleman has said. There are reports that Prime Minister Bazargan has once again tendered his resignation. I think that the right hon[orable] Gentleman is right in his implication that the political situation in Tehran and throughout Iran is likely to remain confused for some time, but that does not alter the obligations on the authorities in Iran to afford protection to diplomats in their capital.

I think that I have already answered the point about oil supplies. It is clearly a major Western interest that we should keep in close touch all the time with our partners and watch carefully and plan against possible developments to our detriment.

> "The political situation . . . throughout Iran is likely to remain confused for some time, but that does not alter the obligations on the authorities in Iran to afford protection to diplomats."

As for diplomacy, we have to make a judgment on whether we want to send British diplomats and their families to Tehran—there are just over 100 people involved—in such an insecure situation. We have taken the view that because Iran will continue to be an important country in the Middle East it is right that we should ask those in our Diplomatic Service to undertake that risk. I believe that that is the correct judgment at the present time.

The Safety of Diplomats

Mr. Speaker: Order. I propose to call one more hon[orable] Member from either side [that is, from the government and the opposition]. This is an extension of Question Time.

Mr. David Price: Following my hon[orable] Friend's reply, will he consider whether it is right to expose to danger the wives and families of British diplomats in exposed posts such as Tehran? May there not be a case for unaccompanied service in those exposed posts?

Mr. Hurd: My hon[orable] Friend has raised an important point about foreign service. The wives and families were brought out of Tehran. They were then allowed to return earlier this year. This is a difficult judgment. It is not sensible to ask people to remain on unaccompanied service in a difficult post for too long. Obviously, if the situation continues to be turbulent, confused and dangerous, this is a judgment that we must look at again.

Mr. Allan Roberts: Does the Minister agree that not only the Shah would be at risk if returning to Tehran, but that many Iranian students in this country would also be at risk, having been here for some time and become Westernised? Will the hon[orable] Gentleman undertake to persuade the Prime Minister and other Ministers to discuss the problem that is now arising as a result of the Government's paranoia about immigration? Deportation notices are now being served on Iranian students who do not want to return, forcing them to return. They are at risk if they return. Would not the Government consider extending to many of these students the well-known British hospitality, in terms of political asylum?

Mr. Hurd: The hon[orable] Gentleman is going very wide of the question. If he has specific points about individuals whom he believes are at risk as a result of their political opinions, I suggest that he raises them with my right hon[orable] Friend the Home Secretary [the minister in charge of domestic affairs].

The United States Fails to Free Its Hostages in Iran

Robert Shaplen

The following viewpoint discusses US president Jimmy Carter's failed efforts to free American hostages captured during the 1979 Iranian Revolution. The author notes that despite deep divisions among his advisors and opposition from allies, Carter approved a military raid to free the hostages. The raid failed, hurting diplomatic efforts. The raid, he says, also undermined the position of those in Iran who hoped to set the hostages free. He concludes that Carter probably should have opted for quiet diplomacy rather than allowing the Iranian crisis to become a high-profile issue and then resorting to force. Robert Shaplen is a former correspondent and staff writer for the New Yorker.

The enormously complicated effort to free the Americans held captive in Iran since November, 1979, which reached a painful climax with the aborted commando raid late in April [1980], not only

SOURCE. Permission granted by the Estate of Robert Shaplen and The New Yorker Magazine.

has been a highly frustrating experience for the many American officials engaged in the protracted diplomatic negotiations but the longer the crisis has lasted the more dramatically it has affected the internal politics and the external relations of both the United States and Iran. In the light of election-year politics here and of the upheaval created by the year-and-a-half-old Iranian revolution, the roles and reputations of [US] President Jimmy Carter and [Iranian] President Abolhassan Bani-Sadr have become important elements in themselves.

The Decision

In the opinion of those who directed the April raid, the chaotic conditions in Iran and the intractable attitudes of Iranian officials—particularly of Ayatollah Ruhollah Khomeini, the remote, messianic figure who is the spiritual fountainhead of the revolution—threatened to bring about the political disintegration of Iran and guarantee its domination by the Soviet Union, which made it urgent to try to extricate the hostages by force. While this opinion was not shared by Secretary of State Cyrus R. Vance and others in the State Department, Zbigniew Brzezinski, the President's national-security adviser, was especially worried about the Russian threat, feeling that the long-term consequences of any Soviet influence in Iran, direct or indirect, would ultimately destroy the balance of forces in the Persian Gulf region. Those who disagreed with this believed that if the raid had been successful, the Iranians might have become angry enough to move further toward an accommodation with the Russians, despite the Soviet invasion of neighboring Afghanistan, to the east; but Brzezinski and others believed that, beyond the overriding national desire to free the hostages, it was important to resolve the crisis—by force, if necessary—so that the United States could at least try to establish some sort of new working relationship with Iran and help avert a civil war there or a conflict between

Iran and its western neighbor, Iraq—either of which would serve the interests of the Russians, who border Iran on the north. Additional factors determined the timing of the raid, including climatic ones; the Pentagon noted that temperatures in the Iranian desert were rising and the Iranian nights were getting shorter—conditions that would soon make helicopter operations difficult and would intensify the risk of detection.

Politically, Carter had at first gained the support of the vast majority of Americans for his policy of patience and restraint in dealing with the hostage problem, but by mid-March he was facing rising criticism from his Republican opponents, Ronald Reagan and George [H.W.] Bush; from his Democratic opponent, Senator Edward Kennedy; from the press and growing portions of the public, including the families of the hostages, who felt that the country was being dishonored and euchred by the Iranians. Carter's decision to go ahead with the raid—which led to the resignation of Secretary Vance—is said to have been the most difficult one of the President's Administration and reflected his own deep anguish over the problem. Some of the critics felt that any raid, if it was to be attempted at all, should have been carried out much sooner, and that once Carter had chosen the path of quiet diplomacy, he should have continued to follow that course, taking successive peaceful steps to put pressure on Iran.

> [US president Jimmy] Carter's decision to go ahead with the raid . . . is said to have been the most difficult one of [his] Administration.

On April 7th, two and a half weeks before the commando attack was mounted, Carter formally broke diplomatic relations with Iran, and ten days later he announced a ban on all exports to Iran, along with steps to seize more than eight billion dollars' worth of previously frozen Iranian assets in the United States and in American banks abroad for payment of claims against

the new revolutionary regime. It was unlikely, as Carter realized, that these mostly symbolic moves would in themselves hasten the release of the hostages—if anything, such economic reprisals promised to make the Iranians more obdurate—but by this time the President was in the position of being damned if he did take stronger measures and damned if he didn't. Publicly,

Iranians holding Americans hostage set a US flag on fire on the roof of the occupied US embassy in Tehran on November 9, 1979. (AP Photo.)

he had all along avoided the use of military force, but in mid-April he went as far as to say that "the only next step available" was "some sort of military action," which was believed to mean a naval blockade or the mining of Iranian harbors.

Actually, having privately made up his mind to go ahead with the raid, he had informed the National Security Council [N.S.C.] of his decision on April 11th, while Secretary Vance was on a four-day vacation in Florida. Deputy Secretary of State Warren Christopher, who attended the N.S.C. meeting in Vance's place, was aware that the Secretary was one of the few key figures in the Administration who knew about the proposed mission. Christopher did not wish to telephone Vance on an open line about the President's decision, but he made sure that the Secretary, upon his return, would be given the opportunity to register his opposition.

Objections to the Proposed Raid

Vance got back to Washington on the fourteenth, and the next day, at a private meeting with Carter, he set forth his objections to the raid strenuously, pointing out that even if it succeeded it would be at the risk of the safety of approximately two hundred other Americans still living in Iran, who might also be seized as hostages. Vance also felt that the raid would jeopardize our tenuous relations in the Persian Gulf area as well as our relations with our allies. The following day, Carter called another meeting of the N.S.C., at which Vance expressed his objections, but the other members of the Council, including Brzezinski, knew that Carter had already made his decision, and Vance was simply listened to politely. On the seventeenth, Vance told Carter that, even if the raid succeeded, he would resign.

> The White House sent out a number of conflicting signals, designed to confuse the Iranians and the world at large by making the imminent use of force appear less likely.

During the following week, the White House sent out a number of conflicting signals, designed to confuse the Iranians and the world at large by making the imminent use of force appear less likely. This happened just as the European Economic Community was voting to support partial sanctions against the Iranians and to institute full sanctions by mid-May unless "decisive progress" was made on the hostage issue. The allies took these steps in an effort to buy more time and to preclude any use of force, which they, too, believed would endanger the larger situation in the Persian Gulf area and pose the threat of a major war there, perhaps further involving the Soviet Union, with which they wanted to maintain some aspects of détente, notwithstanding the [1979 Soviet] invasion of Afghanistan.

When the raid occurred, they were dismayed and disturbed, but they rallied behind Carter and agreed to press ahead with their economic restrictions, although they eventually watered them down to include only transactions entered into after the fourth of November. Behind the scenes, they encouraged new diplomatic approaches to the Iranians, but it seemed doubtful, in the light of the raid and the mixed anger and bravado it had provoked in Iran, whether these fresh efforts would soon come anything like as close to producing a solution to the crisis as had some efforts that were made in the period between late February and early April. . . .

Policy Conflicts in Iran

In Iran, the leading politicians were having problems of a different kind. The efforts of Sadegh Ghotbzadeh, the Foreign Minister, and President Bani-Sadr, both of whom had originally opposed the seizure of the hostages and were eager to get them released so that they could move on to more important matters in the domestic sphere, were being hamstrung by the rigidly conservative Islamic members of Iran's Revolutionary Council;

> Whenever . . . a resolution, or partial resolution, of the crisis seemed possible, Khomeini had refused to budge from his virulent anti-American position.

by the student militants, who from time to time threatened to kill the hostages if the United States took any military action against Iran; and, above all, by Khomeini and his small, tight entourage, sometimes described among critical Iranians as "the bureau." Whenever the chips were down and a resolution, or partial resolution, of the crisis seemed possible, Khomeini had refused to budge from his virulent anti-American position and had come out on the side of the militants and of Bani-Sadr's conservative Islamic enemies.

The most recent example of Khomeini's stubborn, uncompromising behavior was his refusal early in April to approve transfer of control of the hostages, as tentatively approved by Bani-Sadr and Ghotbzadeh, from the militants to the Revolutionary Council, which itself had at first approved the action but then had been unable to reach a decision after a heated second meeting. Even the militants had tentatively agreed to it, but when Khomeini ruled against it, because the Council lacked unanimity, the transfer deal fell through. Khomeini thereupon repeated what he had said earlier—that the not yet fully elected Iranian parliament would have to decide on the fate of the hostages. The second half of the election took place on May 9th, but there was no guarantee that the parliament, dominated by the Islamic Republican Party, which opposes Bani-Sadr, would back down from what has all along been the demand of the Iranians that the deposed Shah, Mohammed Reza Pahlavi, be returned to face trial or that, at least, the billions of dollars he is alleged to have stolen be returned to the revolutionary government.

The Shah is now in Egypt, convalescing after his second serious operation within five months, and the Egyptians have no intention of turning him over to the

Iranians—with whom they have no formal relations. The attitude of the Iranian parliament is not likely to be any more ameliorative as a result of the failed raid and of Carter's having tightened the economic screws on the country. Whether Carter, notwithstanding strong objections by Vance, should have economically done more sooner and cut off shipments of food and medicines, which he exempted from the initial embargo, is a question that is bound to be debated, along with the decision on the raid, as the American election [of 1980] draws closer. Had he done so, the raid might not have taken place when it did. He might have waited until fall, when the weather would again have been favorable, and by then the renewed diplomatic efforts now under way might have been successful enough to obviate the commando attempt.

The Failure of the Raid

The pros and cons of the raid have already become the source of much argument. In Washington, even more than elsewhere, the question that everyone was asking on April 25th, when the failure of the attempt was announced and its details were first disclosed, was "Why now?" Although it was necessary to keep the raid secret, even from the allied leaders, the fact remains that, under pressure from the United States, they had just agreed to sanctions in the belief that force would not be used, and in this sense they were deceived by Carter and the State Department. The cat-and-mouse game played by the White House in an effort to confuse the American public and the Iranians was one thing, but it was something else to exert our diplomatic influence on our allies to further the pretense that we were willing to remain patient and apply continued economic pressure in the interests of a peaceful solution when in reality we were secretly mounting an armed attack dangerous to all concerned.

Our friends abroad had come to feel, as many in this country also had, that while we had every reason to be deeply disturbed about the holding of the hostages against all accepted principles of international law, we had become obsessed by the issue and allowed it to obscure larger common purposes, including the maintenance of peace in the Persian Gulf region. The critics maintained that those purposes might have been better served by simply forgetting about the prisoners, at least publicly, for a time—until the Iranians had sorted out themselves and their untidy revolution and achieved some degree of stability. Despite their awful ordeal, the hostages did not appear to be in any imminent danger, but by constantly attacking the Iranians for holding them so long we simply stoked the revolutionary fires in Iran and further stimulated anti-American passions among the Islamic zealots.

> Quiet diplomacy, the critics said, would have been likely to achieve more than making a fuss about the hostages and turning the whole affair into a carnival of despair.

Quiet diplomacy, the critics said, would have been likely to achieve more than making a fuss about the hostages and turning the whole affair into a carnival of despair. As a former journalist, [David Dunlop] Newsom, who played a leading role in the diplomatic efforts to free the captive Americans, was sympathetic toward the press, but he and others at the State Department regretted the tremendous attention paid to the hostages, since it interfered with the secret negotiations in their behalf; constant telecasts of what was happening in Iran, he felt, offered the militants holding the hostages a perfect platform from which to expound and demonstrate their hatred of the Shah and of the alleged duplicity of America, called by Khomeini "the great Satan." Some thoughtful historians remembered the Pueblo, the American intelligence ship that was seized by the North Koreans in

1968, and—while admitting that the two cases were not altogether comparable, since North Korea was a tightly controlled Communist country, with which it was impossible to negotiate through intermediaries—pointed out that President [Lyndon] Johnson's patient low-key approach led to the freeing of its crew of eighty-two after eleven months through a succession of tortuous face-saving devices: The crew members, under duress, signed confessions, which they later repudiated; the American government simultaneously signed a statement of apology prepared by the North Koreans, and then immediately disavowed it, having told the North Koreans in advance that it would do so.

A number of American and foreign observers felt that an earlier, carefully crafted admission of our powerful role in supporting the Shah for so many years and condoning some of his excesses might have mollified the Iranians and, even though their demand for the Shah's extradition was not met, would have created a better atmosphere for diplomacy to work out a resolution of the crisis. Instead, the raid was undertaken, and when the details were revealed it became clear that if the assault had been fully carried out, and not aborted in the Iranian desert, scores of Iranians might have been injured, or even killed. According to the extremely complicated plan, helicopters were to carry ninety troops the first night to the rendezvous point, outside Teheran, which had been reconnoitred by undercover agents, both American and Iranian. Even if this move had been undetected, the possible use of fighter planes and heavy aerial and ground weaponry to support the commandos if they ran into trouble during the attack on the Embassy the following night, when the troops were to proceed in buses and trucks to the Embassy grounds, would almost surely have caused casualties to numbers of Iranians and might have caused the death of some of the hostages as well. For the commandos to have been able to avoid detection throughout and complete their bold assignment, and then get the freed Americans safely out of the city by helicopters to an airstrip where transport planes were waiting, would have required a vast amount of luck. There was speculation afterward that some Iranian officials had been tipped off to the raid in advance, but the Americans denied this.

Renewed Diplomatic Efforts

Once the raid had failed, the militants announced that the hostages would be dispersed to as many as a dozen cities in Iran. It remains unclear just how many have been dispersed, but in addition to probably reducing the hostages' safety, this would compound the difficulty of negotiating their collective transfer to the custody of the Iranian government as a first step in arranging their freedom. In fact, any fresh diplomatic moves appeared to have been stymied in the immediate weeks following the foiled raid. Now resumed, however, such moves are bound to follow the pattern of earlier almost successful efforts. From the outset, aside from the mutually suspicious American and Iranian officials, the negotiations over the hostages involved a host of other world figures, including Secretary-General Kurt Waldheim of the United Nations and an independent five-man commission of inquiry he appointed to consider Iran's grievances and to visit the prisoners, plus more than a score of other diplomats and private individuals. Foremost among these last were a pair of Paris lawyers representing Iranian interests, who were especially active in getting the U.N. commission to go to Iran late in February and then in trying to arrange the hostages' transfer to the Revolutionary Council in April. Over the past eight

> Even if the hostages are eventually released safely, their long ordeal is likely to leave psychological scars on most of them and on members of their families.

months, this unique diplomatic drama, in which the State Department and the White House played key directing roles, was essentially a shadow play; those behind the scenes were as important as the visible figures, and the performance required much offstage maneuvering; indeed, what took place there was often in direct contrast to what appeared to be happening onstage. There the actors providing the dialogue were forced to keep their true purposes and motivations obscure; the script could well have been written by [absurdist playwright Luigi] Pirandello. Even if the hostages are eventually released safely, their long ordeal is likely to leave psychological scars on most of them and on members of their families and lesser marks on the professional diplomats who have striven over so many nerve-racking months to arrange their freedom.

The Islamic Government in Iran Restricts Women's Rights

Leslie Keith

In the following viewpoint written in the year following the Iranian Revolution, the author explains that the Islamic government is imposing greater restrictions on women's dress. The regime has stated that female government employees must wear a *hijab*, or head scarf. Many women anticipate that this requirement will be extended to all women, the author says. Many Iranians and Iranian women approve of these changes, though there are also middle-class women who have never worn the head scarf and see its imposition as oppressive. Leslie Keith was a writer for the *Christian Science Monitor*.

SOURCE. Leslie Keith, "Iran Reverses Women's 'Liberation' As Muslim Hard-Line Pressures Grow," *Christian Science Monitor*, July 11, 1980. Used by permission.

It's the thin edge of the wedge," said a young Iranian translator in Tehran, brushing her hair into a shawl. "First they will force the women government employees into the hejjab [also spelled *hijab*], and then gradually they will make the rest of us do the same."

The Hejjab and Fundamentalism

She was talking about the Iranian government's efforts to compel women government employees to wear the hejjab (Islamic veil), or at least a head scarf, when at work. Women attempting to protest the move in rallies and street demonstrations and by wearing black as a sign of mourning for their "lost rights" have been more or less silenced.

> In the eyes of Muslim devotees, a lack of 'proper' dress is genuinely felt to be immodest.

Some have lost their jobs. Others have been arrested for demonstrating illegally. The rest have gone to work with head scarves dutifully covering their hair.

The outcome is yet another indication of today's trend toward religious fundamentalism in Iran. The campaign by Westernized and largely middle-class Iranian women to retain and even expand their "liberated" status within the context of Ayatollah Khomeini's Islamic revolution appears to be fizzling out.

The reasons are various.

In the eyes of Muslim devotees, a lack of "proper" dress is genuinely felt to be immodest. Probably the great majority of peasant or working-class Iranian women would concur with such a verdict.

At the same time, Western dress, like most other aspects of Western culture, has become associated with the much vilified regime of the two former shahs. Reza Shah, for instance, father of the monarch ousted last year [in 1979], imposed a "liberation from the veil" half a century ago, often using brutal methods.

He ordered his police to go out into the streets and rip the veils, notably the chadors (long, usually black, head-to-foot shawls leaving only eyes and part of the face uncovered), off any women wearing them. Hundreds of thousands of women thus "liberated" against their will and that of their families and husbands decided to stay that way if only to avoid a second insult in the streets.

The chador later became a symbol of the Khomeini-inspired revolution. Says Sadeq Khalkhali, the controversial Islamic judge:

"It is these Muslim women wearing the chador who helped to bring the revolution to victory. It is they who faced the bullets and tanks of the criminal Shah's forces and defeated them."

The message is clear. The middle-class Iranian women now so bitterly protesting the reimposition of the hejjab were not the ones who fought the revolution. They had better fall into line.

Legislating Dress

"I swear I was there too," said one middle-class Iranian woman to the *Christian Science Monitor*, "out there among those hundreds of thousands of other people. Maybe not during the earlier demonstrations, but later when the numbers swelled I used to take my two children with me and join the demonstrations."

The woman, Zohreh (her name withheld on request), wore no head scarf as she spoke. She was a good example of a middle-class Iranian woman who has never worn any kind of veil since her childhood, whose husband does not want her to wear the hejjab, and who dresses in a typically Western style.

> Her dress was modest by Western standards, but the lack of a head scarf made it 'un-Islamic.'

Her dress was modest by Western standards, but the lack of a head scarf made it "un-Islamic." Zohreh and other middle-class women like her are simply following in the footsteps of their mothers and grandmothers, who were "liberated" initially by Reza Shah.

Under the Khomeini regime's new dress code, all female government office workers have been told to wear a hejjab or veil covering each woman's head, neck, and shoulders. Each must also wear long-sleeved dresses covering her arms up to the wrist. This, the officials explained, will do for the time being, until the President's office and the Revolutionary Council draw up a uniform dress for all women government employees. Such a garment is expected to be the same in design, but not necessarily in color, for all government offices and institutions.

"It could have been worse," said one young government employee. "Thank God they didn't ask us to wear the chador."

On July 6, 1980, a group of women demonstrate outside the Iranian prime minister's offices to protest the requirement that female government employees wear veils. **(Kaveh Kazemi/ Getty Images.)**

Some of the less fundamendalist Iranian clergy-men, such as the late Ayatollah Mahmoud Taleghani, said shortly after the new regime came into existence that calling for the hejjab did not necessarily mean that women would have to wear the chador.

President [Abolhassan] Bani-Sadr says the hejjab helps to maintain the "respect and exalted position of women." This view is echoed by millions of Iranian women, such as Ayatollah Taleghani's daughter, Azam, now a member of the Iranian parliament.

Azam Taleghani believes in veiling herself in the strictest possible manner. She wears a flowing black chador. Yet she still manages to lead a very active political life, addressing public rallies, addressing numerous indoor meetings, and granting interviews to radio, television, and newspaper reporters—many of them men.

CHAPTER 2

Controversies Surrounding the Iranian Revolution

The United States Should Have Supported the Shah More Fully

James Perloff

The following viewpoint argues that the shah modernized Iran and fought against Communist subversion, advancing the interests of the United States, of justice, and of the Iranian people. However, the author says that the US policy establishment, led by the Council on Foreign Relations (CFR), turned against the shah for unknown reasons and used its influence to overthrow him. He suggests that the CFR and the United States may have disliked the shah's nationalization of oil, or some of his mildly anti-Israeli actions. The author concludes that the United States should cease to follow the dictates of the CFR and should stop its activist foreign policy. James Perloff is a freelance writer who has contributed to the *New American*; he is the author of *The Shadows of Power: The Council on Foreign Relations and the American Decline*.

Photo on previous page: A woman guards the US embassy compound during the hostage crisis in November 1979. The role of women in society was severely restricted in the years following the revolution. **(AP Photo/ Mohammad Sayad.)**

SOURCE. James Perloff, "Iran and the Shah: What Really Happened," *New American*, May 12, 2009. Used by permission.

From 1941 until 1979, Iran was ruled by a constitutional monarchy under Mohammad Reza Pahlavi, Iran's Shah (king).

The Shah and Modernization

Although Iran, also called Persia, was the world's oldest empire, dating back 2,500 years, by 1900 it was floundering. Bandits dominated the land; literacy was one percent; and women, under archaic Islamic dictates, had no rights.

The Shah changed all this. Primarily by using oil-generated wealth, he modernized the nation. He built rural roads, postal services, libraries, and electrical installations. He constructed dams to irrigate Iran's arid land, making the country 90-percent self-sufficient in food production. He established colleges and universities, and at his own expense, set up an educational foundation to train students for Iran's future.

To encourage independent cultivation, the Shah donated 500,000 Crown acres to 25,000 farmers. In 1978, his last full year in power, the average Iranian earned $2,540, compared to $160 25 years earlier. Iran had full employment, requiring foreign workers. The national currency was stable for 15 years, inspiring French economist André Piettre to call Iran a country of "growth without inflation." Although Iran was the world's second largest oil exporter, the Shah planned construction of 18 nuclear power plants. He built an Olympic sports complex and applied to host the 1988 Olympics (an honor eventually assigned Seoul), an achievement unthinkable for other Middle East nations.

> At the height of Iran's prosperity, the Shah suddenly became the target of an ignoble campaign led by U.S. and British foreign policy makers.

Long regarded as a U.S. ally, the Shah was pro-Western and anti-communist, and he was aware that he posed the main barrier to Soviet ambitions in the Middle East. . . . The Shah's air force ranked among the world's five best. A voice for stability within the Middle East itself, he favored peace with Israel and supplied the beleaguered state with oil.

On the home front, the Shah protected minorities and permitted non-Muslims to practice their faiths. "All faith," he wrote, "imposes respect upon the beholder." The Shah also brought Iran into the 20th century by granting women equal rights. This was not to accommodate feminism, but to end archaic brutalization.

Yet, at the height of Iran's prosperity, the Shah suddenly became the target of an ignoble campaign led by U.S. and British foreign policy makers. Bolstered by slander in the Western press, these forces, along with Soviet-inspired communist insurgents, and mullahs opposing the Shah's progressiveness, combined to face him with overwhelming opposition. In three years he went from vibrant monarch to exile (on January 16, 1979), and ultimately death, while Iran fell to Ayatollah Khomeini's terror.

The United States Works Against the Shah

Houchang Nahavandi, one of the Shah's ministers and closest advisers, reveals in his book *The Last Shah of Iran*: "We now know that the idea of deposing the Shah was broached continually, from the mid-seventies on, in the National Security Council in Washington, by Henry Kissinger, whom the Shah thought of as a firm friend."

Kissinger virtually epitomized the American establishment: before acting as Secretary of State under Republicans Richard Nixon and Gerald Ford, he had been chief foreign-affairs adviser to Nelson Rockefeller, whom he called "the single most influential person in my life." Jimmy Carter defeated Ford in the 1976 presidential election, but the switch to a Democratic administration did not change the new foreign policy tilt against the Shah. Every presidential administration since Franklin D. Roosevelt's has been dominated by members of the Council on Foreign Relations (CFR), the most visible manifestation of the establishment that dictates U.S. foreign policy along internationalist lines. The Carter administration was no exception. . . .

[By the late 1970s], the Shah noted, the U.S. media found him "a despot, an oppressor, a tyrant." [US Senator Ted] Kennedy denounced him for running "one of the most violent regimes in the history of mankind."

At the center of the "human rights" complaints was the Shah's security force, SAVAK. Comparable in its mission to America's FBI, SAVAK was engaged in a deadly struggle against terrorism, most of which was fueled by the bordering USSR, which linked to Iran's internal communist party, the Tudeh. SAVAK, which had only 4,000 employees in 1978, saved many lives by averting several bombing attempts. Its prisons were open for Red Cross inspections, and though unsuccessful attempts were made on the Shah's life, he always pardoned the would-be assassins. Nevertheless, a massive campaign was deployed against him. Within Iran, Islamic fundamentalists, who resented the Shah's progressive pro-Western views, combined with Soviet-sponsored communists to overthrow the Shah. This tandem was "odd" because communism is committed to destroying *all* religion, which Marx called "the opiate of the masses." The Shah understood that "Islamic Marxism" was an oxymoron, commenting: "Of course the two concepts are irreconcilable—unless those who profess Islam do not understand their own religion or pervert it for their own political ends."

> Comparable in its mission to America's FBI, SAVAK was engaged in a deadly struggle against terrorism, most of which was fueled by the bordering USSR.

For Western TV cameras, protestors in Teheran carried empty coffins, or coffins seized from genuine funerals, proclaiming these were "victims of SAVAK." This deception—later admitted by the revolutionaries—was necessary because they had no actual martyrs to parade. Another tactic: demonstrators splashed themselves with mercurochrome, claiming SAVAK had bloodied them.

The Western media cooperated. When Carter visited Iran at the end of 1977, the press reported that his departure to Teheran International Airport had been through empty streets, because the city was "all locked up and emptied of people, by order of the SAVAK." What the media didn't mention: Carter chose to depart at 6 A.M., when the streets were naturally empty.

An equally vicious campaign occurred when the Shah and his wife, Empress Farah, came for a state visit to America in November 1977. While touring Williamsburg, Virginia, about 500 Iranian students showed up, enthusiastically applauding. However, about 50 protestors waved hammer-and-sickle red flags. These unlikely Iranians were masked, unable to speak Persian, and some were blonde. The U.S. media focused exclusively on the protesters. Wrote the Shah: "Imagine my amazement the next day when I saw the press had reversed the numbers and wrote that the fifty Shah supporters were lost in a hostile crowd." . . .

Terror at Home

Two major events propelled the revolution in Iran. On the afternoon of August 19, 1978, a deliberate fire gutted the Rex Cinema in Abadan, killing 477 people, including many children with their mothers. Blocked exits prevented escape. The police learned that the fire was caused by Ruhollah Khomeini supporters, who fled to Iraq, where the ayatollah was in exile. But the international press blamed the fire on the Shah and his "dreaded SAVAK." Furthermore, the mass murder had been timed to coincide with the Shah's planned celebration of his mother's birthday; it could thus be reported that the royal family danced while Iran wept. Communist-inspired rioting swept Iran.

Foreigners, including Palestinians, appeared in the crowds. Although the media depicted demonstrations as "spontaneous uprisings," professional revolutionaries organized them. Some Iranian students were caught up in it. Here the Shah's generosity backfired. As [foreign affairs specialist Hillaire] du Berrier pointed out:

> In his desperate need of men capable of handling the sophisticated equipment he was bringing in, the Shah had sent over a hundred thousand students abroad. . . . Those educated in France and America return indoctrinated by leftist professors and eager to serve as links between comrades abroad and the Communist Party at home.

When the demonstrations turned violent, the government reluctantly invoked martial law. The second dark day was September 8. Thousands of demonstrators gathered in Teheran were ordered to disperse by an army unit. Gunmen—many on rooftops—fired on the soldiers. The Shah's army fired back. The rooftop snipers then sprayed the crowd. When the tragedy was over, 121 demonstrators and 70 soldiers and police lay dead. Autopsies revealed that most in the crowd had been killed by ammo non-regulation for the army. Nevertheless, the Western press claimed the Shah had massacred his own people.

> "Khomeini had denounced the Shah's reforms during the 1960s—especially women's rights and land reform for Muslim clerics, many of whom were large landholders."

The Shah, extremely grieved by this incident, and wanting no further bloodshed, gave orders tightly restricting the military. This proved a mistake. Until now, the sight of his elite troops had quieted mobs. The new restraints emboldened revolutionaries, who brazenly insulted soldiers, knowing they could fire only as a last resort.

Meanwhile, internationalist forces rallied around a new figure they had chosen to lead Iran: Ruhollah Khomeini. A minor cleric of Indian extraction, Khomeini had denounced the Shah's reforms during the 1960s—especially women's rights and land reform for Muslim clerics, many of whom were large landholders. Because his incendiary remarks had contributed to violence and rioting then, he was exiled, living mostly in Iraq, where Iranians largely forgot him until 1978.

A shadowy past followed Khomeini. The 1960s rioting linked to him was financed, in part, by Eastern Bloc intelligence services. He was in the circle of the cleric Kachani Sayed Abolghassem, who had ties to East German intelligence. Furthermore, in 1960, Colonel Michael Goliniewski, second-in-command of Soviet counter-intelligence in Poland, defected to the West. His debriefings exposed so many communist agents that he was honored by a resolution of the U.S. House of Representatives. One report, declassified in 2000, revealed, "Ayatollah Khomeini was one of Moscow's five sources of intelligence at the heart of the Shiite [Muslim denomination] hierarchy."

> Within Iran 'the Voice of America, the Voice of Israel and, especially, the BBC virtually became the voice of the revolution, moving from criticism to overt incitement of revolt.'

Nevertheless, as French journalist Dominique Lorenz reported, the Americans, "having picked Khomeini to overthrow the Shah, had to get him out of Iraq, clothe him with respectability and set him up in Paris, a succession of events which could not have occurred, if the leadership in France had been against it."

In 1978, Khomeini, in Iraq since 1965, was permitted to reside at Neauphle-le-Château in France. Two French police squads, along with Algerians and Palestinians, protected him. . . .

Journalists descended in droves on Neauphle-le-Château; Khomeini gave 132 interviews in 112 days, receiving easy questions as their media organs became his sounding board. Nahavandi affirms that, within Iran "the Voice of America, the Voice of Israel and, especially, the BBC [US and Israeli government radio, and public radio of Great Britain] virtually became the voice of the revolution, moving from criticism to overt incitement of revolt, and from biased reporting to outright disinformation."

Khomeini's inflammatory speeches were broadcast; revolutionary songs aired on Iranian radio. One journalist, however, stunned Khomeini by bucking the trend: intelligence expert Pierre de Villemarest, hero of the French Resistance in World War II, anti-communist, and critic of the CFR. Interviewing Khomeini, de Villemarest asked:

> How are you going to solve the economic crisis into which you have plunged the country through your agitation of these past few weeks? . . . And aren't you afraid that when the present regime is destroyed you will be outpaced by a party as tightly-knit and well organized as the [Communist] Tudeh?

Khomeini didn't reply. The interpreter stood, saying, "The Ayatollah is tired." De Villemarest registered his concern with the French Ministry of the Interior, but reported, "They told me to occupy myself with something else."

Ending the Shah's Rule

Iran's situation deteriorated. As Western media spurred revolutionaries, riots and strikes paralyzed Iran. The Shah wrote:

> At about this time, a new CIA chief was stationed in Teheran. He had been transferred to Iran from a post

in Tokyo with no previous experience in Iranian affairs. Why did the U.S. install a man totally ignorant of my country in the midst of such a crisis? I was astonished by the insignificance of the reports he gave me. At one point we spoke of liberalization and I saw a smile spread across his face.

> [The shah] finally accepted exile, clinging to the belief that America was still Iran's ally, and that leaving would avert greater bloodshed.

The Carter administration's continuous demand upon the Shah: liberalize. On October 26, 1978, he freed 1,500 prisoners, but increased rioting followed. The Shah commented that "the more I liberalized, the worse the situation in Iran became. Every initiative I took was seen as proof of my own weakness and that of my government." Revolutionaries equated liberalization with appeasement. "My greatest mistake," the Shah recalled, "was in listening to the Americans on matters concerning the internal affairs of my kingdom."

Iran's last hope: its well-trained military could still restore order. The Carter administration realized this. Du Berrier noted: "Air Force General Robert Huyser, deputy commander of U.S. forces in Europe, was sent to pressure Iran's generals into giving in without a fight." "Huyser directly threatened the military with a break in diplomatic relations and a cutoff of arms if they moved to support their monarch."

"It was therefore necessary," the Shah wrote, "to neutralize the Iranian army. It was clearly for this reason that General Huyser had come to Teheran."

Huyser only paid the Shah a cursory visit, but had three meetings with Iran's revolutionary leaders—one lasting 10 hours. Huyser, of course, had no authority to interfere with a foreign nation's sovereign affairs.

Prior to execution later by Khomeini, General Amir Hossein Rabbi, commander-in-chief of the Iranian Air

Force, stated: "General Huyser threw the Shah out of the country like a dead mouse."

U.S. officials pressed the Shah to leave Iran. He reflected:

> You cannot imagine the pressure the Americans were putting on me, and in the end it became an order.... How could I stay when the Americans had sent a general, Huyser, to force me out? How could I stand alone against Henry Precht [the State Department director for Iran] and the entire State Department?

He finally accepted exile, clinging to the belief that America was still Iran's ally, and that leaving would avert greater bloodshed. These hopes proved illusions.

A factor in the Shah's decision to depart was that—unknown to most people—he had cancer. U.S. Ambassador William Sullivan (CFR) assured the Shah that, if he exited Iran, America would welcome him. Despite the pleadings of myriad Iranians to stay, he reluctantly left. However, shortly after reaching Cairo, the U.S. ambassador to Egypt effectively informed him that "the government of the United States regrets that it cannot welcome the Shah to American territory."

The betrayed ruler now became "a man without a country."

Ayatollah Khomeini Takes Power

On February 1, 1979, with U.S. officials joining the welcoming committee, Ayatollah Khomeini arrived in Iran amid media fanfare. Although counter-demonstrations, some numbering up to 300,000 people, erupted in Iran, the Western press barely mentioned them.

Khomeini had taken power, not by a constitutional process, but violent revolution that ultimately claimed hundreds of thousands of lives. Numerous of his opponents were executed, usually without due process, and often after brutal torture. Teheran's police officers—loyal to the Shah—were slaughtered. At least 1,200 Imperial Army officers, who had been instructed by General Huyser not to resist the revolution, were put to death. Before dying, many exclaimed, "God save the King!" "On February 17," reported du Berrier, "General Huyser faced the first photos of the murdered leaders whose hands he had tied and read the descriptions of their mutilations." At the year's end, the military emasculated and no longer a threat, the Soviet Union invaded Afghanistan. More Iranians were killed during Khomeini's first month in power than in the Shah's 37-year reign. Yet Carter, Ted Kennedy, and the Western media, who had brayed so long about the Shah's alleged "human rights" violations, said nothing. Mass executions and torture elicited no protests. Seeing his country thus destroyed, the exiled Shah raged to an adviser: "Where are the defenders of human rights and democracy now?" Later, the Shah wrote that there was:

> Why did the American establishment, defying logic and morality, betray our ally the Shah?

> not a word of protest from American human rights advocates who had been so vocal in denouncing my "tyrannical" regime! It was a sad commentary, I reflected, that the United States, and indeed most Western countries, had adopted a double standard for international morality: anything Marxist, no matter how bloody and base, is acceptable. . . .[1]

Oil and Israel

Why did the American establishment, defying logic and morality, betray our ally the Shah? Only the perpetrators can answer the question, but a few possibilities should be considered.

Iran ranks second in the world in oil and natural-gas reserves. Energy is critical to world domination, and

Some argue that accomplishments such as the Dez Dam, which provides water and electricity for Iran, should have resulted in stronger support for the shah. (James P. Blair/ National Geographic/ Getty Images.)

major oil companies, such as Exxon and British Petroleum, have long exerted behind-the-scenes influence on national policies.

The major oil companies had for years dictated Iranian oil commerce, but the Shah explained:

> In 1973 we succeeded in putting a stop, irrevocably, to sixty years of foreign exploitation of Iranian oil-resources. . . . In 1974, Iran at last took over the management of the entire oil-industry, including the refineries at Abadan and so on. . . . I am quite convinced that it was from this moment that some very powerful, international interests identified, within Iran, the collusive elements, which they could use to encompass my downfall.

Does this explain the sudden attitude change toward Iran expressed by Henry Kissinger, beginning in the mid-seventies? Kissinger's links to the Rockefellers, whose fortune derived primarily from oil, bolsters the Shah's view on the situation. However, other factors should be considered.

Although the Shah maintained a neutral stance toward Israel, during the 1973 Yom Kippur War, he allowed critical supplies to reach Egypt, enabling it to achieve a balance of success, and earning Sadat's undying gratitude, but wrath from influential Zionists. Did this impact the West's attitude change in the mid-seventies?

We should not overlook that the Shah opposed the powerful opium trade, now flourishing in the Middle East.

Finally, the Shah was a nationalist who brought his country to the brink of greatness and encouraged Middle East peace. These qualities are anathema to those seeking global governance, for strong nations resist membership in world bodies, and war has long been a destabilizing catalyst essential to what globalists call "the new world order."

What is the solution to modern Iran? Before listening to war drums, let us remember:

It was the CFR clique—the same establishment entrenched in the [US presidents George W.] Bush and [Barack] Obama administrations—that ousted the Shah, resulting in today's Iran. That establishment also chanted for the six-year-old Iraq War [begun in 2003] over alleged weapons of mass destruction never found. Therefore, instead of contemplating war with Iran, a nation four times Iraq's size, let us demand that America shed its CFR hierarchy and their interventionist policy that has wrought decades of misery, and adopt a policy of avoiding foreign entanglements, and of minding our own business in international affairs.

Note

1. The shah was a committed anti-Marxist and felt that Marxist forces had been responsible for his overthrow.

The United States Should Not Have Supported the Shah

Anonymous

The *Harvard Crimson* is the student newspaper of Harvard University. In this viewpoint from the paper, anonymous Iranian students argue a few months after the Iranian Revolution that the shah's regime was brutal and oppressive. They say the shah's secret police were engaged in a massive campaign of murder and torture against dissenters. The authors also state that the shah used the military against his own people and prevented minority groups from studying their own culture. The authors conclude that allowing the shah asylum in the United States is against American principles and justice, and that he should be extradited to Iran to face punishment for his crimes.

It was indeed a strange episode when the Shah of Iran, former head of one of the world's most brutal and repressive states, managed to land in the U.S. as

SOURCE. "Life Under the Shah," *The Harvard Crimson*, December 6, 1979. Used by permission of The Harvard Crimson.

a "private citizen." For several days leading newspapers published first page stories detailing the treatment of the Shah's cancer, creating a mood conducive to accepting him on humanitarian grounds. Only a few months earlier the press and the U.S. Senate were raising hell about the execution of the Shah's military chiefs and ex-cronies in Iran. They complained bitterly about the violation of due process of law. But they conveniently forgot that the Shah's own military courts (which were unconstitutional) tried as terrorists anyone brave enough to protest his regime. The verdict was often decided beforehand. Where were the passionate defenders of law then?

> "The Shah systematically dismantled the judicial system of Iran and the country's guarantees of personal and social liberties."

The Shah systematically dismantled the judicial system of Iran and the country's guarantees of personal and social liberties. His regime consistently violated the codes of law and justice, destroying the dignity of our people by treating them like backward savages to be pulled with an iron hand out of the middle ages into the light of the modern era. Nearly every source of creative, artistic and intellectual endeavor in our culture was suppressed.

The media said little about the 80 percent of peasant families remaining landless, about the growing shanty towns holding the displaced peasants, the misery and alienation of these people ripped from their traditional way of life and subject to new economic and cultural pressures.

The media had less to say about the 60 per cent of adults left illiterate, and the increasing income gap which made Iran one of the world's most unequal societies. Little was heard about the royal family's financial scandals and their heroin smuggling on a global scale.

SAVAK conducted most of the torture, under the friendly guidance of the CIA, which set up SAVAK

in 1957 and taught them how to interrogate suspects. Amnesty International reports methods of torture that included "whipping and beating, electric shocks, extraction of teeth and nails, boiling water pumped into the rectum, heavy weights hung on the testicles, tying the prisoner to a metal table heated to a white heat, inserting a broken bottle into the anus, and rape."

The Shah greatly expanded the military and turned it against his own people. With newfound oil wealth the Shah bought $2C million of U.S. arms. The U.S. military trained Iranian officers. Despite claims that a strong army was needed to prevent external aggression, its real purpose became clear last year when the army murdered more than 50,000 Iranians fighting the Shah (the number is based on estimates of dead quickly buried after street massacres and compiled throughout the year).

At Tehran's main cemetery on December 19, 1978, relatives hold up photos of family members who they claim died from torture inflicted by Iran's secret police. (**AP Photo/IVE.**)

Under the Shah education was a means of pacification. Our history books were full of lies about the glories of the Iranian dynasties, and they encouraged racism towards non-Persian-speaking minorities in Iran as well as nearby nations. A special military guard was stationed on most large university campuses to mute student opposition. The number of students tortured, lost or murdered is unknown. Yet the universities remained a bulwark of opposition to the Shah and his cultural aggression.

> The Shah's presence in the U.S. is a disgrace and an insult to the integrity of the American people.

The national minorities in Iran have fared even worse. Millions of Kurds, Turks, Arabs, Baloochis and Turkamans were deprived of the right to learn in their mother tongues, and no cultural expression or publication was allowed in their languages.

Our people have experienced enormous physical and spiritual suffering under the Shah. Today he and his top generals, the worst murderers of all, are in this country, protected by its laws. Meanwhile innocent Iranian students are harassed and singled out for deportation. If existing laws can be amended overnight to intimidate Iranian students, why cannot the same laws be changed to require the extradition of criminals like the Shah?

The Shah's presence in the U.S. is a disgrace and an insult to the integrity of the American people, regardless of their view on the hostage issue. The conflict is not between our nations. Our anger is not directed at Americans because they are Americans. We have no genes for anti-Americanism in us. Our anger is directed at those in power who installed and maintained the Shah for 25 years, as they still do for dictators in Chile, Guatemala, Paraguay, the Philippines and around the world.

Sentiments for war are running high on both sides. We must resist these tendencies because the costs to everyone are too high. We appeal to your integrity and intelligence to raise your voices against the presence of a criminal of monstrous proportions in this country, if not for sympathy for the Iranian people, for the values you aspire to yourselves.

The Western Press Unfairly Demonized the Iranian Revolution

Edward W. Said

In the following viewpoint, a Palestinian American scholar argues that in the year after the Iranian Revolution, the American press presented stereotypes about Islam and disinformation about the revolution itself. He notes that the American press claimed that Iranians desired martyrdom and suggested that Islam was irrational. The press spent little time, he asserts, discussing the recent history of Iran, the cruelty of the shah's dictatorship, or the reasons that the revolution in Iran was popular. Instead the revolution was seen as an unmotivated insult to the United States. Said suggests that the treatment of the revolution in the American press was motivated by prejudice and self-interest. Edward W. Said was a professor of English and comparative literature at Columbia University and the author of *Orientalism*.

SOURCE. Edward W. Said, "Iran and the Press: Whose Holy War?" *Columbia Journalism Review*, v. 18, no. 6, March-April, 1980. Used by permission.

To sift through the immense amount of material generated by the embassy occupation in Tehe-ran on November 4, 1979 [when revolutionaries took American hostages], is to be struck by a number of things. For one, it seemed that "we" were at bay, and, with "us," the normal, democratic, rational order of things. Out there, writhing in self-provoked frenzy, was "Islam," whose manifestation of the hour was a disturbingly neu-rotic Iran.

The Press Attacks Islam

The press found plenty of evidence to substantiate this view. On November 7 the *St. Louis Post-Dispatch* printed the proceedings of a seminar held in St. Louis on Iran and the Persian Gulf. One participating expert was quoted as saying that "the loss of Iran to an Islamic form of government was the greatest setback the United States has had in recent years." Islamic self-governance, in other words, is by definition inimical to U.S. interests. *The Wall Street Journal* editorialized on November 20 that "civilization is receding" due to "the decline of the Western powers that spread these [civilized] ideals to begin with," as if not to be Western—which is the fate of most of the world's popula-tion, and Islam's to boot—is not to have had any civi-lized ideals. All the major TV commentators, Walter Cronkite and Frank Reynolds chief among them, spoke of "anti-Americanism" or more poetically of "the cres-cent of crisis, sweeping across the world of Islam like a cyclone hurtling across a prairie," as ABC's Reynolds put it on November 21; on December 7 he voiced over a picture of crowds chanting "God is great" with what he supposed was the crowd's true sentiment, "hatred of America."

> It became necessary [for the US media] to attack our antago-nists, to deprecate their beliefs and belittle their customs.

If we were thus at bay, it became necessary to attack our antagonists, to deprecate their beliefs and belittle their customs. Later in the same December broadcast, ABC informed us that the prophet Mohammed was "a self-proclaimed prophet" (which prophet hasn't been?) and then reminded us that "Ayatollah" was "a self-styled twentieth-century title" meaning "reflection of God" (both, unfortunately, not completely accurate accounts). The ABC short (three-minute) course on Islam was held in place with small titles to the right of the picture, and they told the same story of how resentment, suspicion, and contempt were proper for "Islam," which was reduced to a rush of images and symbols: Mecca, Purdah, Chador, Sunni, Shi'ite (accompanied by a picture of young men beating themselves), Mullah, Ayatollah, Khomeini, Iran. Soon after this rapid-fire sequence, the program switched to Jamesville, Wisconsin, whose admirably wholesome schoolchildren—no purdah [the Islamic practice of concealing women from men], self-flagellation, or mullahs here—were organizing a patriotic "Unity Day."

After more than a year's worth of journalistic enterprise on the subject—which included the December 11 publication of a symposium of scholars and experts—any lingering doubts about what we were to think about Islam were cleared up when, in the last four days in December, *The New York Times* published a series of long articles by Flora Lewis, all attempting a serious treatment of "Upsurge in Islam," in the words of the running head. (*The New Republic* had already gone to the limit in the rhetoric of headlines, tying together two December 8 articles by Walter Laqueur and Michael Walzer with "The Holy Wars of Islam.") There are some excellent things in Lewis's pieces—for example, her success in delineating complexity and diversity—but there are serious weaknesses, too, most of them inherent in the way Islam is viewed nowadays. Not only did Lewis single out Islam from other religions in the Middle East (the upsurge in Judaism and Egyptian or Lebanese Christianity, for instance, was scarcely mentioned), but she went on to make statements, in particular in her third story, about the Arabic language (quoting expert opinion that its poetry is "rhetorical and declamatory, not intimate and personal") and the Islamic mind (an inability to employ "step-by-step thinking") that would be considered either racist or nonsensical if used to describe any other language, religion, or combination of ethnic groups. Too frequently her authorities were orientalists well known for their rancorous general views: one of them, Elie Kedourie, of the London School of Economics, is quoted as saying that "the disorder of the east is deep and endemic"; Bernard Lewis, the Princeton orientalist, pronounces on "the end of free speculation and research" in the Islamic world, presumably as a result of Islam's "static" as well as its "determinist, occasionalist and authoritarian" theology. One could not be expected to get a coherent view of Islam after reading Flora Lewis—her scurrying about in sources and her unfamiliarity with the subject give her readers the sense of a scavenger hunt for a subject that wasn't one to begin with; after all, how could one get hold of the remarkably varied history, geography, social structure, and culture of forty Islamic nations and 800,000,000 people whose words "are an expression of wish rather than a description of fact"? The point about Islam was made, anyway, that even if "it" wasn't clear at all, one's attitudes toward it were.

Innuendo and Incrimination

There were subtler ways to incriminate "Islam." One was to put an expert before the public and have him or her suggest that [Ayatollah] Khomeini was not really "representative of Islamic clergy" (this was L. Dean Brown, former U.S. ambassador to Jordan and special envoy to Lebanon and now president of the Middle East Institute,

History Cannot Be Swept Clean

I wish I could say . . . that general understanding of the Middle East, the Arabs, and Islam in the United States has improved somewhat, but alas, it really hasn't. For all kinds of reasons, the situation in Europe seems to be considerably better. In the United States, the hardening of attitudes, the tightening of the grip of demeaning generalization and triumphalist cliché, the dominance of crude power allied with simplistic contempt for dissenters and "others" has found a fitting correlative in the looting, pillaging, and destruction of Iraq's libraries and museums [following the 2003 invasion of Iraq]. What our leaders and their intellectual lackeys seem incapable of understanding is that history cannot be swept clean like a blackboard, clean, so that "we" might inscribe our own future there and impose our own forms of life for these lesser people to follow. It is quite common to hear high officials in Washington and elsewhere speak of changing the map of the Middle East, as if ancient societies and myriad peoples can be shaken up like so many peanuts in a jar. But this has often happened with the "Orient" [the East including the Middle East], that semi-mythical construct, which, since Napoleon's invasion of Egypt in the late eighteenth century, has been made and remade countless times by power acting through an expedient form of knowledge to assert that this is the Orient's nature, and we must deal with it accordingly. In the process the uncountable sediments of history, which include innumerable histories and a dizzying variety of peoples, languages, experiences, and cultures, all these are swept aside or ignored, relegated to the sand heap along with the treasures ground into meaningless fragments that were taken out of Baghdad's [Iraq's capital] libraries and museums. My argument is that history is made by men and women, just as it can also be unmade and rewritten, always with various silences and elisions, always with shapes imposed and disfigurements tolerated, so that "our" East, "our" Orient becomes "ours" to possess and direct.

SOURCE. *Edward W. Said,* Orientalism. *New York: Random House, 1979 (preface 2003), p. xviii.*

speaking on [PBS news program] *The MacNeil/Lehrer Report*, November 16), that the "ironclad" mullah was a throw-back to an earlier (obviously Islamic) age, and that the mobs in Teheran [Iran's capital] were reminiscent of Nuremberg [i.e., Nazi rallies], just as the street demonstrations were signs of the "circus as principal entertainment" habitually provided by dictators.

Another method was to suggest invisible lines connecting various other Middle Eastern things to Iranian Islam, then to damn them together, implicitly or explicitly, depending on the case. When former Senator James Abourezk went to Teheran, the announcement on ABC and CBS was made with a reminder that Abourezk was "of Lebanese origin." No reference was ever made to Representative George Hansen's Danish background, or to Ramsey Clark's WASP ancestry. Somehow it was considered important to disclose the vaguely Islamic taint in Abourezk's past, although he happens to be of Christian Lebanese stock.

Much [of] the most flamboyant use of suggestion originated in a small front-page item by Daniel B. Drooz in *The Atlanta Constitution* on November 8, in which it was alleged that the Palestine Liberation Organization [or PLO, which seeks the creation of an independent Palestinian state free of Israeli control] was behind the embassy takeover. His sources were authorities in "diplomatic and European intelligence." (Coming in a close second was his November 22 discovery that "Where there are Shi'ites [the Muslim denomination most prevalent in Iran], there is trouble.") A month later George Ball stated gnomically in *The Washington Post* that "there is some basis to believe that the whole operation is being orchestrated by well-trained Marxists." Not to be outdone, CBS introduced its *Evening News* on December 12 with Marvin Kalb from the State Department quoting (equally unnamed) "diplomatic and intelligence experts" as affirming that Palestinian guerrillas, Iranian extremists, and Islamic fundamentalists had cooperated at the embassy. The PLO men were the ones who had mined the compound, Kalb said; they

> Surprisingly . . . one has the feeling of not having learned very much from all of this reporting [on the Iranian crisis].

were known to be inside, he went on sagely, by virtue of "the sounds of Arabic" being heard from the embassy. (A brief report of Kalb's "story" was carried the next day in the *Los Angeles Times*.) It remained for no less a personage than Hudson Institute expert Constantine Menges to argue exactly the same thesis first in *The New Republic* of December 15, then twice more on *The MacNeil/Lehrer Report*. No more evidence was given; it sufficed to conjure up the diabolism of communism in natural alliance with the devilish PLO and satanic Moslems.

Surprisingly, given the hundreds of hours of broadcast coverage and the millions of words in newspapers and magazines, one has the feeling of not having learned very much from all of this reporting. The media certainly provided abundant evidence of their power to be there, in Teheran, and of their knack for prodding events into assimilable, if rudimentary, shape. But there was no help to be had in analyzing the complicated politics of what was taking place. Returning to the U.S. after a trip abroad, Vermont Royster commented in *The Wall Street Journal* of December 19 that the accumulated pile of newspapers and TV programs he started going through testified to:

> how little I learned about the Iranian crisis [that] I didn't already know, despite the voluminous coverage given it. Once home I was startled to find myself inundated in a daily tidal wave of television, radio and newspaper stories about Iran. The papers carried long stories under huge headlines, while TV devoted most of the evening news to the topic and then ran late-evening specials almost every night.
>
> And from that arose another heretical thought, that the news media were engaged in overkill.
>
> This may seem a strange reaction about a story of such obvious importance. . . . But the volume of words to tell a story doesn't necessarily equate with informa-

tion imparted. The truth is that in much of that wordage there was no real news at all.

Stereotypes Rather than News

The news was the same; so was the narrow and quickly exhausted range of assumptions used to look for it. How long is it possible to rely on experts and reporters who are understandably concerned about the hostages, incensed at the impropriety of the thing, perhaps also angry at Islam, and still hope to get fresh information, news, analysis? If one were to read the *Chicago Tribune* on November 18—a piece by James Yuenger, citing experts who said that "this is not something that's up for rational discussion" or that Iranians have a "tendency to look for scapegoats" and "a sort of hunger for martyrdom"—and then either *Time* ("An Ideology of Martyrdom") or *Newsweek* ("Iran's Martyr Complex") the week after, and almost any paper of one's choice the week after that, one would continually keep coming up against the information that Iranians are Shi'ites who long for martyrdom, who are led by a nonrational Khomeini, who hate our country, are determined to destroy the satanic spies, are unwilling to compromise, and so forth.

> Was there no Iranian history or society to write and speak about that *wasn't* translatable into the anthropomorphisms of a crazy Iran gratuitously taunting good-guy America?

Were there no events taking place in Iran *before* the embassy takeover that might illuminate things? Was there no Iranian history or society to write and speak about that wasn't translatable into the anthropomorphisms of a crazy Iran gratuitously taunting good-guy America? Above all, was the press simply interested in diffusing news seemingly in keeping with a U.S. government policy to keep America "united" behind the unconditional demand for the hostages' release, a demand shrewdly

Young men about to leave for the Iran-Iraq war self-flagellate and wear white shrouds as a gesture of martyrdom at an assembly in Tehran. Some critics say that the Western press relied on images like this one to perpetuate stereotypes about Islam and to demonize the Iranian Revolution. (Kaveh Kazemi/Getty Images.)

assessed by Roger Fisher of Harvard on the December 3 *Today* show as being itself subordinate to the real priority, which was not freeing the hostages but maintaining "the prestige and power of the United States"?

Anyone saturated with superficial, loose-tongued reporting on Iran would be prone to turn for relief and genuine insight to the nightly *MacNeil/Lehrer Report*. But the programs—with their restrictive (and even conservative) format, choice of guests, and range of discussion—were unsatisfying at their best and mystifying at their worst.

Given an unconventional news story about as unfamiliar a part of the world as Iran, the viewer will immediately be made to feel an intense disparity between the Middle Eastern mobs and the program's carefully dressed, carefully selected cast of guests, whose uniform qualification was dispassionate expertise, not necessarily insight or understanding. The questions asked made it evident that *MacNeil/Lehrer* tended to be looking for support of the prevailing national mood—outrage at the Iranians—both by eliciting ahistorical analyses of what makes the Iranians tick and by guiding discussion to fit either Cold War or crisis-management molds. A telling indication of this appeared in the two programs (December 28 and January 4) on which the guests were the two sets of American clergymen recently returned from Teheran. On both programs the clergymen told of their obvious compassion for Iranians who had suffered under the ex-shah's despotic rule for twenty-five years. Lehrer was openly skeptical, not to say dubious, about what they were saying. When Foreign Minister Abolhassan Bani-Sadr and his successor Sadegh Ghotbzadeh appeared (November 23 and 29), the line of questioning stayed very close to what had emerged as the U.S. government position: when will the hostages be released, [Robert] MacNeil and [Jim] Lehrer wanted to know, and never mind talk of concessions or committees to investigate the ex-shah's misdemeanors and crimes.

> Few guests [on television news and talk shows] could truly communicate the essentially 'foreign' language of distant, oppressed people who until now had silently endured decades of American impingement on their lives.

The Government Line

The guest list was significant. Aside from the five appearances by Iranians, and two by supporters of Third-World and antiwar causes, most of the other panelists on the score of shows devoted to the crisis were newspapermen, government officials, academic Middle East experts, individuals connected to corporate or quasi-governmental institutions, and Middle Easterners known for their essentially antagonistic positions on the Iranian revolution. The discussions resulting from this lineup usually placed everything the Iranians said and did out of moral bounds, since few guests could truly communicate the essentially "foreign" language of distant, oppressed people who until now had silently endured decades of American impingement on their lives. Neither Lehrer nor MacNeil, moreover, tried to investigate what Bani-Sadr meant when, evoking "the oppressed people of the world," he suggested that satisfaction of their claims did not demand the ex-shah's extradition, but required only a gesture of recognition from the U.S. that the oppressed had legitimate grievances.

Thus, in the very conduct of its investigation The *MacNeil/Lehrer Report* seemed to censor itself, prevent itself from straying into wider areas of human experience that antagonists or interlocutors thought were important. The questions invariably focused on how to deal with the crisis (not with trying to understand the new horizons being hewed out everywhere in the nonwhite, non-European world); the answers seemed to resort almost instinctively to received wisdom about sectarian unrest, Islamic revivalism, geopolitics, balance of power. These were the constraints within which MacNeil and Lehrer operated. And for better or for worse, they happen to be the very constraints within which the government itself operated.

In the context of such cautious and conformist journalism, we can now begin to appreciate the astonishing prescience of I.F. Stone's piece "A Shah Lobby Next?" which he wrote over a year ago and which was published in *The New York Review of Books* of February 22, 1979. He spoke there of how the ex-shah, who had just left Iran, could "rally formidable friends" from the Chase Manhattan Bank, the arms industry, the oil trust, the CIA, and "hungry academia" to get an American visa. Were he to be admitted to the U.S., Stone speculated, tempting possibilities might arise, even though "we should have learned by now, but haven't, to keep out of Iran's domestic politics, and we may get a parallel lesson soon in keeping Iran's politics out of ours." Why? Because, Stone's uncanny predictions continued:

> What if the new Iranian regime makes demands of its own. . . . lays claim—as Khomeini has already indicated—to the foreign holdings and bank accounts of the Shah and the Pahlavi Foundation? What if it demands the Shah's return for trial on charges of plundering his country? . . . What if it accuses him, as absolute ruler, with absolute responsibility for untold tortures and deaths at the hands of SAVAK [the Iranian secret police]?

American Interests

Stone not only happens to have been right; he is not, and has never pretended to be, an "expert" on Iran. Look through his article and you will find no reference to the Islamic mentality, or Shi'ite predilections for martyrdom, or any of the other nonsense parading as relevant "information" on Iran. He understands politics, he understands and makes no attempt to lie about what moves men and women to act in this society, as well as all others. Above all, he does not doubt that even though Iranians are not Europeans or Americans, they may have legitimate grievances, ambitions, and hopes of their own, which it would be folly for us to ignore.

> "Iranians . . . have legitimate grievances, ambitions, and hopes of their own, which it would be folly for us to ignore."

With characteristic hardheadedness, syndicated columnist Joseph Kraft sketched *his* very different view of the matter in "Time for a Show of Power," which appeared in *The Washington Post* on November 11. It was what he wrote there, far more than all the standard reporting about diplomatic immunity and the sanctity of our embassy, that illuminated aspects of the underlying, perhaps even unconscious, rationale behind the news media's overall performance. The downfall of the shah, Kraft wrote, was "a calamity for American national interests." Not only did the shah make available regular supplies of oil; he imposed order on the Iranian plateau through "his imperial pretensions." This was good for America: it kept the oil flowing, of course; it kept the region, as well as "submerged nationalities," in line; it kept "us" appearing strong. Kraft went on to recommend, as part of the process of "rebuilding American policy toward Iran," that the U.S. find occasion "for an unmistakable, and preferably surprising, assertion of American power." How might this be done?

> [It] might take the form of supporting Iraq in its effort to stir up provincial resistance inside Iran. It might mean giving military assistance to Turkey.... The United States needs a capacity to do something besides sending Marines and bombing. It has to rebuild a capacity self-destructed only a few years ago—a capacity for covert intervention.

What is clear in Kraft's piece is his unwillingness to accept the Iranian revolution as ever having taken place; everything connected to it must be destroyed as the aberration he wanted his readers to believe it was. In other words, Kraft was projecting his personal version of reality onto a complex Iranian as well as American reality, thereby substituting his wishes for the facts. Kraft's version had the additional didactic merit of being entirely devoid of morality: it was about power, American power to have the world on our terms, as though twenty-five years of intervention in Iran had taught us nothing. If in the process Kraft found himself denying that other people have a right to produce a change in their own form of government, denying even that a change had definitively taken place, that did not much matter. He wanted America to know (and be known by) the world through its power, its needs, its vision. All else was an outrage.

The Western Press Was Correct About the Dangers of the Iranian Revolution

David Zarnett

In the following viewpoint, a British writer argues that left-wing intellectuals such as Edward Said failed to see the real nature of the Iranian Revolution. He says that the Western media, on the other hand, did a fairly good job of interpreting the revolution. In particular, he says, the media in the West took the statements of the Ayatollah Khomeini seriously. As a result, the media correctly reported on the repressive and Islamic nature of the revolutionary regime, he argues. Said and other leftists, on the other hand, downplayed both the Islamic character of the revolution and its human rights abuses. David Zarnett is studying political science at the University of Toronto.

SOURCE. David Zarnett, "Edward Said and the Iranian Revolution," *Democratiya 9*, Summer 2007. Reprinted with permission of the University of Pennsylvania Press.

The Iranian revolution was not only a godsend for those Muslims who identified with its cause, it was also a blessing for those among the American Left who saw it as a significant blow against the evil American Empire. For them it was a non-violent resurgence of the oppressed of the Third-World, noble and progressive in its cause and buoyed by its religious character. Richard Falk in *The Nation* wrote 'the religious core of the Khomeini movement is a call for social justice, fairness in the distribution of wealth, a productive economy organized around national needs and simplicity of life and absence of corruption that minimizes differences between rich and poor, rulers and ruled.' The fears expressed by Iranian leftists and feminists were an exaggeration and not worthy of pause or consideration. That Tehran's bookstores were selling books once banned by the Shah and that newspapers were engaging in lively political debate was sufficient proof that the inherent progressive forces of the revolution would prevail. 'Whatever the future course of this remarkable revolution,' Kai Bird wrote in *The Nation*, 'the spring of 1979 is budding with hopes of broader freedoms and economic well-being for the Iranian people.'

The Left Deludes Itself

What led so many on the left to predict utopia in Iran after the overthrow of the Shah? This essay will seek part of the explanation in [Palestinian American scholar] Edward Said's influential analysis of the Iranian Revolution. It is a locus of some key errors—of denial, evasion, and abstract categorial thinking immune to the facts—that led to such a gross miscalculation on the part of so many American Leftists.

Said's analysis negated two realities. The first reality was the one

> Said's analysis negated two realities. The . . . one reported by the American mainstream media . . . [and] the words written and spoken by Ayatollah Khomeini.

reported by the mainstream American media. One assumption that underpinned Said's analysis was that the media's portrayal of the revolution must be inherently wrong and that the truth must lie in a 'counter-narrative.' That Said was neither an expert on Middle Eastern politics nor the history of Islam; that he knew little of the Shah or Ayatollah Khomeini beyond what an informed layman would have known; and that he did not read or write Farsi, makes his utter conviction concerning the inaccuracy of the media's portrayal all the more indicative of his method of analysis and thought. The second reality that Said negated was the words written and spoken by Ayatollah Khomeini, notably in *Velayat-e Faqeeh* (Islamic Government), and the clues they provided for the future path of the Iranian Revolution. Khomeini's belief that the Jews were bent on world domination and that Shari'a [Islamic] law would create an ideal society was purposefully kept out of Said's analysis. This same approach was taken by Richard Falk, who dismissed Khomeini's writings as having little significance because they were 'disavowed by Khomeini's closest advisors.' Instead Falk saw it more appropriate to rely on Khomeini's utterances to Western visitors and journalists claiming that the earliest critics of Khomeini were simply supporters of the Shah and nothing more. . . .

The Media and Khomeini

The revolution in Iran thrust 'Islam' into mainstream discourse in America. From his residence-in-exile in Neauphle-le-Chateau on 12 January, 1979, Ayatollah Khomeini stated that the 'struggle will continue until the establishment of an Islamic Republic that guarantees the freedom of the people, the independence of the country, and the attainment of social justice.' A few months later, in his hometown of Qom, Khomeini declared the establishment of the Islamic Republic, calling on the new government to 'enact Islamic justice under the banner of Islam and the flag of the Qur'an.' These statements received much publicity and Khomeini's words were widely circulated through major news outlets. Taking its cue from Khomeini's rhetoric, the American media began to portray the revolution as religiously inspired, which gave rise to a concerned debate about the implications of this new political ideology rooted in Islam. Specifically, Khomeini's declaration to establish an 'Islamic Republic' begged the question of what such a polity would look like. *The Washington Post* predicted a political catastrophe based on a reading of excerpts of Khomeini's *Velayat-e Faqeeh*. *The Associated Press* and *Time* followed suit (the cover of *Time Magazine* of 16 April, 1979 read: 'Islam: The Militant Revival'). In the pages of the *New Republic*, Michael Walzer, in an article Said specifically attacked, depicted Khomeini as a clerical fascist and wrote of the need to 'remind ourselves of the power of one religion still capable of generating great zeal among large numbers of its followers.' In *Foreign Affairs,* where the early analysis had generally minimized the role of Islam in the revolution, William Quandt depicted Khomeini as more concerned with the 'Great Satan' than with the significant and numerous domestic problems plaguing post-Shah Iran. Similar to Walzer, Quandt noted that 'one of the questions that surrounded the Iranian Revolution from its onset was whether Khomeini and his Islamic Republic might signal a new resurgence of Islamic feeling and solidarity that would affect other Islamic nations, especially those in the Middle East.'

After his years of research and writing for his book *Orientalism* (1978), Said thought he knew exactly what was going on. His analysis of systematic Western misperceptions of Islam—orientalism—was to be vindicated by a stinging critique of this orientalist discourse about the Iranian revolution. His critique would draw heavily upon his earlier writings. In a 1976 review of *The Cambridge History of Islam* (1970), edited by Said's arch-nemesis Bernard Lewis, Said described this widely respected book as an anti-Islamic diatribe void of 'ideas and methodological intelligence.' In *Orientalism*, which reproduces this review of *History* almost verbatim, Said emphasised that the work's central point revolves around the question of what defines the Muslim human experience: '*Orientalism*, however, clearly posits the Islamic category (over the socio-economic category) as the dominant one, and this is the main consideration about [*History*'s] retrograde intellectual tactics.' In other words, to an orientalist, Muslims were only Muslims and not economic, political and rational beings, so their revolutions could not be rational political acts. . . .

Said believed that the media's misrepresentation of Khomeini was due to ignorance: 'why did no reporter seem to avail himself of crucial material contained in the Summer 1979 issue of *Race and Class*—for example, the material on Ali Shariati, an Iranian friend of Algerian revolutionary Frantz Fanon, who with Khomeini was the major influence on the revolution?' This point raises two important questions. First, if Said had versed himself in Iranian revolutionary ideology as he demands of journalists reporting and writing on Iran, why did he not once cite the writings of Shariati or Khomeini and pass on any of this required information to his readers? Second, if Khomeini is indeed a 'major influence on the revolution,' is it not understandable to be deeply concerned with Khomeini's political agenda considering the ideas and political programme presented in his major work *Velayat-e Faqeeh*? Even if Hamid Algar's translation of *Velayat-e Faqeeh* was not yet available to Said at the time of writing this article—Algar's work first appeared in 1981—*The Washington Post* published excerpts in February 1979, making its core ideas widely ac-

> Even *The Nation*, who early in 1979 was committed to viewing Khomeini as a progressive, was beginning to realize their error in judgement.

cessible. Perhaps it was for this very reason—that it was published in a mainstream media outlet—that Said, and many others who believed Khomeini to be a progressive, failed to take into consideration Khomeini's own words.

Said's defence of Khomeini came at a time of mounting evidence against him and his leadership. Even *The Nation*, who early in 1979 was committed to viewing Khomeini as a progressive, was beginning to realize their error in judgement. Still clinging to its optimism about the revolution, *The Nation* asked its readership not to associate the current human rights violations under Khomeini with the revolution itself. Said, however, was distinct in this regard and did not budge from his position—his hostility to the media threw off his moral compass. Reports of human rights abuses, executions, and violent atrocities committed by Khomeini and other Iranians in the name of the revolution were greatly exaggerated for obvious reasons: 'More important, reporters and editors have clearly favoured stories reporting atrocities, executions, and ethnic conflict over those of the country's extremely fluid, actually quite open, political struggle. . . . If aggressive hyperbole is one journalistic mode commonly used to describe Iran, the other is misapplied euphemism, usually stemming from ignorance, but often deriving from a barely concealed ideological hostility.'

Attacking the Media

Eventually, under the weight of growing criticism of Khomeini by members within his own leftist milieu, Said succumbed to reality. But he did not shift to take a strong stance against Khomeini nor write urgently and in detail about the atrocities being committed. Instead, Said evaded reality by focusing on the US media's characterization of the Iranian revolution as 'Islamic.' . . .

In his article, 'Islam Through Western Eyes,' published in *The Nation* in April 1980, Said does show that

Iranians wait in line outside Tehran's Qasr Prison in May 1979 to visit relatives being held by the revolutionary government. Some argue that the Western press was correct in anticipating human rights abuses such as excessive imprisonment after the revolution. **(AP Photo.)**

the excesses of Khomeini are no longer defensible: 'What is the Islamist apologist to say when confronted with the daily count of people executed by the Islamic Komitehs or when—as reported on September 19, 1979 by Reuters—Ayatollah Ruhollah Khomeini announces that enemies of the Islamic revolution would be destroyed?' However, his primary argument is that the revolution's excesses can not be explained simply by invoking the all-encompassing adjective of 'Islam.' He attacked the American obsession with Islam arguing that 'no non-Western realm has been so dominated by the United States as the Arab-Islamic world is dominated today.' America lacked sympathy for Islam: 'in the United States, at least, there is no major segment of the polity, no significant sector of the culture, no part of the whole community capable of identifying sympathetically with the Islamic World.' And because of this hostility, figures like Khomeini typify an Islamic world seen as being 'populated by shadowy (although extremely frightening) notions about jihad, slavery, subordination of women and irrational violence combined with extreme licentiousness.' Conversely, Anwar Sadat was fashioned in the media as the ideal Muslim 'whose remark that Khomeini was a lunatic and a disgrace to Islam was repeated ad nauseam.' Therefore, Said thought, American perceptions of Islam were defined by American interests. When American interests are not at stake, Islam was of little concern, but when these interests were challenged it was because the all-encompassing Islamic menace reared its head. In this case, Said emphasized the dangers of associating events in Iran to Islam because this approach would negate the nature of the American presence in the region and the legitimate and intense political grievance it creates. Lacking an appreciation for complexity and nuance, Said countered the media's narrative by denying the Iranian revolution an Islamic quality entirely. But as the late Malcolm Kerr once wrote: 'Does Said realize how insistently Islamic doctrine in its many variants has traditionally proclaimed the applicability of religious standards to all aspect of human life, and the inseparability of man's secular and spiritual destinies? What does he suppose the Ayatollah Khomeini and Muslim Brotherhood were all about?'

'Inside Islam: How the Press Missed the Story in Iran,' was published in *Harper's Magazine* in January 1981. A critique of 'The Islam Explosion,' by Michael Walzer, it provides a particularly clear example of Said's method. Said asserted that 'Walzer has convinced himself that when he says the word Islam he is talking about a real object called Islam, an object so immediate as to make any mediation of qualifications applied to it seem supererogatory fussiness.' However, Said's charge that Walzer saw Islam 'as a single thing' simply misrepresents Walzer. Contrary to Said's charge, Walzer warns his

> When defending Khomeini, Said showed no understanding of the major themes that were at the centre of many of the Ayatollah's writings and lectures.

reader against conflating Islam into a single entity and insists on the need to consider local conditions when interpreting conflicts throughout the region. More importantly, and again characteristic of his style of argumentation, Said does not refute Walzer's argument with a counter-argument but with only a swift waving of his hand. What we can see clearly now is that—and note this is an inversion of Said's narrative of 'orientalist' western intellectuals—while Walzer takes heed of what Muslims in the Middle East are saying, Said ignores them.

Said's analysis marginalized Khomeini in two ways. First, when defending Khomeini, Said showed no understanding of the major themes that were at the centre of many of the Ayatollah's writings and lectures. In effect Said ignored Khomeini's ideas. Second, when Khomeini could no longer be defended, Said resorted to simply bracketing his existence and preeminent role in the new Iranian state. In 1982, Said, alongside Richard Falk, personally endorsed a public statement by the 'The Emergency Committee for the Defense of Democracy and Human Rights in Iran,' which, while lambasting the Iranian regime for its human rights abuses and anti-democratic practices, curiously makes no mention of Khomeini. And it was in a 1984 eulogy of the French post-modernist Michel Foucault, who had a great influence on Said, in which he dedicated only a few sentences to the philosopher's very public endorsement of Khomeini and his revolutionary politics that was by no means marginal to his intellectual career, as Said himself admits.

It is not surprising that Said came to a gravely mistaken conclusion of a watershed event in the modern Middle East. His argumentation was not based on expertise or a careful consideration of the evidence available but on the theoretical category of 'orientalism.' His out-of-hand rejection of the media's characterization of the revolution as 'Islamic' resulted from his a priori hostility to all American mainstream media discussions of Islam. His method blocked a more nuanced approach that might have

'Just because you read something in the *Daily Telegraph* doesn't mean it's wrong.'

seen the Islamic *and* the political dimensions of the revolution. It would have served Said well to consider one of [English author] George Orwell's dictums: 'Just because you read something in the *Daily Telegraph* doesn't mean it's wrong.'

The Islamic Revolution Promised Political Spirituality for All

Michel Foucault

In the following viewpoint written in 1978, a leading French intellectual discusses the options for Iranians in the months before the return of the Ayatollah and the exile of the shah. He notes that many in the West hope that Iran will move towards a democratic, parliamentary style of government. He says, however, that Iranians themselves talk of an Islamic government, probably led by the Ayatollah Khomeini, and that the Iranian government may open the way for more spiritual politics, founded on ancient ideals of justice. He suggests that this will benefit all Iranians and perhaps allow them to resist the imperial ambitions of the West. Michel Foucault was an influential social theorist and philosopher perhaps best known for groundbreaking critical studies of social institutions.

SOURCE. Michel Foucault, "What Are the Iranians Dreaming About?" *Foucault and the Iranian Revolution: Gender and Seductions,* University of Chicago Press, 2005. Used by permission of The University of Chicago Press.

They [the United States] will never let go of us [Iran] of their own will. No more than they did in [the 1955–1975 war in] Vietnam." I wanted to respond that they are even less ready to let go of you than Vietnam because of oil, because of the Middle East. Today [1978] they seem ready, after Camp David [i.e., the 1978 peace treaty between Egypt and Israel] to concede Lebanon to Syrian domination and therefore to Soviet influence, but would the United States be ready to deprive itself of a position that, according to circumstance, would allow them to intervene from the East or to monitor the peace?

Internal Liberalization

Will the Americans push the shah toward a new trial of strength, a second "Black Friday" [September 8, 1978, when the Shah's forces shot protestors in Iran]? The recommencement of classes at the university, the recent strikes, the disturbances that are beginning once again, and next month's religious festivals, could create such an opportunity. The man with the iron hand is [Nasser] Moghadam, the current leader of the SAVAK [Iranian secret police].

This is the backup plan, which for the moment is neither the most desirable nor the most likely. It would be uncertain: While some generals could be counted on, it is not clear if the army could be. From a certain point of view, it would be useless, for there is no "communist threat": not from outside, since it has been agreed for the past twenty-five years that the USSR would not lay a hand on Iran; not from inside, because hatred for the Americans is equaled only by fear of the Soviets.

Whether advisers to the shah, American experts, regime technocrats, or groups from the political opposition (be they the National Front [a secular, democratic Iranian party] or more "socialist-oriented" men), during these last weeks everyone has agreed with more or less

Jews in Iran

Reza Shah was the first Iranian monarch in 1,400 years to pay respect to the Jews by praying to the Torah and bowing in front of it, when visiting the Jewish community of Isfahan. An act that boosted the self-esteem of the Iranian Jews and made Reza Shah the second most respected Iranian leader among Jews after Cyrus the Great [founder of the Persian Empire]. . . .

The Islamic Revolution of 1979 made Shariat [Islamic law] the legal code and therefore gender and religious discrimination has become an integral part of the system. Bahais . . . are not recognized at all, but Jews, Christians and Zoroastrians each have one or two representatives in the Parliament and are not legally forbidden from employment in the government sector. They are accepted into universities, but are usually not given access to post graduate studies, though no law prohibits it. There were 85,000 Iranian Jews before 1979, but almost half have emigrated since, mainly to the U.S.— the largest exodus from Iran since Darius' time [1400 B.C.] when 30,000 left joyfully to rebuild their temple.

SOURCE. *Massoume Price, "Ups and (Mostly) Downs: The History of the Jews in Iran," The Iranian, May 12, 2000. www.iranian.com.*

good grace to attempt an "accelerated internal liberalization," or to let it occur. At present, the Spanish model [liberalization following the death of dictator Francisco Franco in 1975] is the favorite of the political leadership. Is it adaptable to Iran? There are many technical problems. There are questions concerning the date: Now, or later, after another violent incident? There are questions concerning individual persons: With or without the shah? Maybe with the son, the wife? Is not former prime minister [Ali] Amini, the old diplomat pegged to lead the operation, already worn out?

> There arose [in Iran] an immense movement from below, which exploded this year, shaking up the political parties that were being slowly reconstituted.

There are substantial differences between Iran and Spain, however. The failure of economic development in Iran prevented the laying of a basis for a liberal, modern, westernized regime. Instead, there arose an immense movement from below, which exploded this year, shaking up the political parties that were being slowly reconstituted. This movement has just thrown half a million men into the streets of Tehran [the Iranian capital], up against machine guns and tanks.

Not only did they shout, "Death to the Shah," but also "Islam, Islam, Khomeini, We Will Follow You," and even "Khomeini for King."

Khomeini Will Not Go Away

The situation in Iran can be understood as a great joust under traditional emblems, those of the king and the saint, the armed ruler and the destitute exile, the despot faced with the man who stands up bare-handed and is acclaimed by a people. This image has its own power, but it also speaks to a reality to which millions of dead have just subscribed.

The notion of a rapid liberalization without a rupture in the power structure presupposes that the movement from below is being integrated into the system, or that it is being neutralized. Here, one must first discern where and how far the movement intends to go. However, yesterday in Paris, where he had sought refuge, and in spite of many pressures, Ayatollah Khomeini "ruined it all."

He sent out an appeal to the students, but he was also addressing the Muslim community and the army, asking that they oppose in the name of the Quran and in the name of nationalism these compromises concerning elections, a constitution, and so forth.

Is a long-foreseen split taking place within the opposition to the shah? The "politicians" of the opposition try to be reassuring: "It is good," they say. "Khomeini, by raising the stakes, reinforces us in the face of the shah and the Americans. Anyway, his name is only a rallying cry, for he has no program. Do not forget that, since 1963, political parties have been muzzled. At the moment, we are rallying to Khomeini, but once the dictatorship is abolished, all this mist will dissipate. Authentic politics will take command, and we will soon forget the old preacher." But all the agitation this weekend around the hardly clandestine residence of the ayatollah in the suburbs of Paris, as well as the coming and going of "important" Iranians, all of this contradicted this somewhat hasty optimism. It all proved that people believed in the power of the mysterious current that flowed between an old man who had been exiled for fifteen years and his people, who invoke his name.

> People believed in the power of the mysterious current that flowed between an old man who had been exiled for fifteen years and his people, who invoke his name.

The nature of this current has intrigued me since I learned about it a few months ago, and I was a little weary, I must confess, of hearing so many clever experts repeating: "We know what they don't want, but they still do not know what they want."

Photo on following page: Revolutionaries hoped for a government more open to spiritual concerns led by Ayatollah Khomeini (center). (**Keystone/ Getty Images.**)

What Do the Iranian People Want?

"What do you want?" It is with this single question in mind that I walked the streets of Tehran and Qom in the days immediately following the disturbances. I was careful not to ask professional politicians this question. I chose instead to hold sometimes-lengthy conversations

with religious leaders, students, intellectuals interested in the problems of Islam, and also with former guerilla fighters who had abandoned the armed struggle in 1976 and had decided to work in a totally different fashion, inside the traditional society.

"What do you want?" During my entire stay in Iran, I did not hear even once the word "revolution," but four out of five times, someone would answer, "An Islamic government." This was not a surprise. Ayatollah Khomeini had already given this as his pithy response to journalists and the response remained at that point.

What precisely does this mean in a country like Iran, which has a large Muslim majority but is neither Arab nor Sunni [a denomination of Islam prevalent throughout the Middle East] and which is therefore less susceptible than some to Pan-Islamism or Pan-Arabism?

Indeed, Shiite Islam [a denomination of Islam prevalent in Iran] exhibits a number of characteristics that are likely to give the desire for an "Islamic government" a particular coloration. Concerning its organization, there is an absence of hierarchy in the clergy, a certain independence of the religious leaders from one another, but a dependence (even a financial one) on those who listen to them, and an importance given to purely spiritual authority. The role, both echoing and guiding, that the clergy must play in order to sustain its influence—this is what the organization is all about. As for Shi'ite doctrine, there is the principle that truth was not completed and sealed by the last prophet. After Muhammad, another cycle of revelation begins, the unfinished cycle of the imams [priests or Islamic leaders], who, through their words, their example, as well as their martyrdom, carry a light, always the same and always changing. It is this light that is capable of illuminating the law from the inside. The latter is made not only to be conserved, but also to release over time the spiritual meaning that it holds. Although invisible before his promised return, the Twelfth

Imam is neither radically nor fatally absent. It is the people themselves who make him come back, insofar as the truth to which they awaken further enlightens them.

It is often said that for Shi'ism, all power is bad if it is not the power of the Imam. As we can see, things are much more complex. This is what Ayatollah Shariatmadari [a leading religious leader in Iran both before and after the revolution] told me in the first few minutes of our meeting: "We are waiting for the return of the Imam, which does not mean that we are giving up on the possibility of a good government. This is also what you Christians are endeavoring to achieve, although you are waiting for Judgment Day." As if to lend a greater authenticity to his words, the ayatollah was surrounded by several members of the Committee on Human Rights in Iran when he received me.

> By 'Islamic government,' nobody in Iran means a political regime in which the clerics would have a role of supervision or control.

One thing must be clear. By "Islamic government," nobody in Iran means a political regime in which the clerics would have a role of supervision or control. To me, the phrase "Islamic government" seemed to point to two orders of things.

Islamic Utopia

"A utopia," some told me without any pejorative implication. "An ideal," most of them said to me. At any rate, it is something very old and also very far into the future, a notion of coming back to what Islam was at the time of the Prophet, but also of advancing toward a luminous and distant point where it would be possible to renew fidelity rather than maintain obedience. In pursuit of this ideal, the distrust of legalism seemed to me to be essential, along with a faith in the creativity of Islam.

A religious authority explained to me that it would require long work by civil and religious experts, scholars, and believers in order to shed light on all the problems to which the Quran never claimed to give a precise response. But one can find some general directions here: Islam values work; no one can be deprived of the fruits of his labor; what must belong to all (water, the subsoil) shall not be appropriated by anyone. With respect to liberties, they will be respected to the extent that their exercise will not harm others; minorities will be protected and free to live as they please on the condition that they do not injure the majority; between men and women there will not be inequality with respect to rights, but difference, since there is a natural difference. With respect to politics, decisions should be made by the majority, the leaders should be responsible to the people, and each person, as it is laid out in the Quran, should be able to stand up and hold accountable he who governs.

> Between men and women there will not be inequality with respect to rights, but difference, since there is a natural difference.

It is often said that the definitions of an Islamic government are imprecise. On the contrary, they seemed to me to have a familiar but, I must say, not too reassuring clarity. "These are basic formulas for democracy, whether bourgeois or revolutionary," I said. "Since the eighteenth century now, we have not ceased to repeat them, and you know where they have led." But I immediately received the following reply: "The Quran had enunciated them way before your philosophers, and if the Christian and industrialized West lost their meaning, Islam will know how to preserve their value and their efficacy."

When Iranians speak of Islamic government; when, under the threat of bullets, they transform it into a slogan of the streets; when they reject in its name, perhaps at the risk of a bloodbath, deals arranged by parties and politicians, they have other things on their minds than these formulas from everywhere and nowhere. They also have other things in their hearts. I believe that they are thinking about a reality that is very near to them, since they themselves are its active agents.

It is first and foremost about a movement that aims to give a permanent role in political life to the traditional structures of Islamic society. An Islamic government is what will allow the continuing activity of the thousands of political centers that have been spawned in mosques and religious communities in order to resist the shah's regime. I was given an example. Ten years ago, an earthquake hit Ferdows. The entire city had to be reconstructed, but since the plan that had been selected was not to the satisfaction of most of the peasants and the small artisans, they seceded. Under the guidance of a religious leader, they went on to found their city a little further away. They had collected funds in the entire region. They had collectively chosen places to settle, arranged a water supply, and organized cooperatives. They had called their city Islamiyeh. The earthquake had been an opportunity to use religious structures not only as centers of resistance, but also as sources for political creation. This is what one dreams about [songe] when one speaks of Islamic government.

But one dreams [songe] also of another movement, which is the inverse and the converse of the first. This is one that would allow the introduction of a spiritual dimension into political life, in order that it would not be, as always, the obstacle to spirituality, but rather its receptacle, its opportunity, and its ferment. This is where we encounter a shadow that haunts all political and religious life in Iran today: that of [Iranian revolutionary and sociologist] Ali Shariati, whose death two years ago gave him the position, so privileged in Shi'ism, of the invisible Present, of the ever-present Absent.

During his studies in Europe, Shariati, who came from a religious milieu, had been in contact with leaders of the Algerian Revolution [against French occupation], with various left-wing Christian movements, with an entire current of non-Marxist socialism. (He had attended [sociologist Georges] Gurvitch's classes.) He knew the work of [French Marxist Franz] Fanon and [French scholar of Islam, Louis] Massignon. He came back to Mashhad [a city in Iran], where he taught that the true meaning of Shi'ism should not be sought in a religion that had been institutionalized since the seventeenth century, but in the sermons of social justice and equality that had already been preached by the first imam. His "luck" was that persecution forced him to go to Tehran and to have to teach outside of the university, in a room prepared for him under the protection of a mosque. There, he addressed a public that was his, and that could soon be counted in the thousands: students, mullahs, intellectuals, modest people from the neighborhood of the bazaar, and people passing through from the provinces. Shariati died like a martyr, hunted and with his books banned. He gave himself up when his father was arrested instead of him. After a year in prison, shortly after having gone into exile, he died in a manner that very few accept as having stemmed from natural causes. The other day, at the big protest in Tehran, Shariati's name was the only one that was called out, besides that of Khomeini.

> Islamic government . . . impressed me in its attempt to open a spiritual dimension in politics.

Political Will

I do not feel comfortable speaking of Islamic government as an "idea" or even as an "ideal." Rather, it impressed me as a form of "political will." It impressed me in its effort to politicize structures that are inseparably social and religious in response to current problems. It also impressed me in its attempt to open a spiritual dimension in politics.

In the short term, this political will raises two questions:

1. Is it sufficiently intense now, and is its determination clear enough to prevent an "Amini solution," which has in its favor (or against it, if one prefers) the fact that it is acceptable to the shah, that it is recommended by the foreign powers, that it aims at a Western-style parliamentary regime, and that it would undoubtedly privilege the Islamic religion?

2. Is this political will rooted deeply enough to become a permanent factor in the political life of Iran, or will it dissipate like a cloud when the sky of political reality will have finally cleared, and when we will be able to talk about programs, parties, a constitution, plans, and so forth?

Politicians might say that the answers to these two questions determine much of their tactics today.

With respect to this "political will," however, there are also two questions that concern me even more deeply.

One bears on Iran and its peculiar destiny. At the dawn of history, Persia invented the state and conferred its models on Islam. Its administrators staffed the caliphate. But from this same Islam, it derived a religion that gave to its people infinite resources to resist state power. In this will for an "Islamic government," should one see a reconciliation, a contradiction, or the threshold of something new?

The other question concerns this little corner of the earth whose land, both above and below the surface, has strategic importance at a global level. For the people who inhabit this land, what is the point of searching, even at the cost of their own lives, for this thing whose possibility we have forgotten since the Renaissance and the great crisis of Christianity, a *political spirituality*. I can already hear the French laughing, but I know that they are wrong.

The Islamic Revolution Betrayed Women

Donna M. Hughes

The following viewpoint argues that women were active participants in the 1979 revolution. The author says that women hoped
they would have greater freedom in a new Iran than under the
shah's oppressive regime. Instead, the Ayatollah Khomeini and
his Islamist government curtailed women's rights, she says. These
restrictions have continued even under supposedly moderate
leaders like Ayatollah Ali Khamenei. The writer notes that women
must abide by a restrictive dress code, are not allowed to travel
without their husband's permission, have few custody or inheritance rights, and are generally separated from men in a strict and
oppressive system of gender apartheid. Donna M. Hughes is a
professor of women's studies at the University of Rhode Island.

SOURCE. Donna M. Hughes, "Women in Iran—A Look at
President Khatami's First Year in Office," *Z Magazine*, October, 1998.
Used by permission of the author.

W omen in Iran want equality, respect and the right to participate in all social, political and economic activities. They want to live their lives productively and with dignity. Throughout the 20th Century Iranian women have organized and fought for human and political rights, from the Constitutional Revolution at the turn of the century to the democratic movement that overthrew the Shah of Iran.

> *Once in power, the fundamentalists betrayed the work and humanity of women by implementing a crushing system of gender apartheid.*

Gender "Apartheid"

Iranian women were strong participants in the 1979 revolution, but fundamentalists, led by Ayatollah Ruhollah Khomeini, seized control after the revolution. Once in power, the fundamentalists betrayed the work and humanity of women by implementing a crushing system of gender apartheid. Fundamentalists built their theocracy on the premise that women are physically, intellectually and morally inferior to men, which eclipses the possibility of equal participation in any area of social or political activity. Biological determinism prescribes women's roles and duties to be child bearing and care taking, and providing comfort and satisfaction to husbands.

Men were granted the power to make all family decisions, including the movement of women and custody of the children. "Your wife, who is your possession, is in fact, your slave," [as judiciary chief Mohammad Yazdi said in 1986] is the mullah's legal view of women's status. The misogyny of the mullahs made women the embodiment of sexual seduction and vice. To protect the sexual morality of society, women had to be covered and banned from engaging in "immodest" activity.

Based on these woman-hating principles, Khomeini and his followers crafted laws and policies that are still [as of 1998] in effect. The hejab, or dress code, is

mandatory in all public places for all women. Women must cover their hair and body except for their face and hands and they must not use cosmetics. Punishments range from a verbal reprimand to 74 lashes with a whip to imprisonment for one month to a year. Stoning to death is a legal form of punishment for sexual misconduct. Women are banned from pursuing higher education in 91 of 169 fields of study and must be taught in segregated classrooms. A woman may work with her husband's permission, although many occupations are forbidden to women.

The legal age at which girls can be married is 9 years (formerly 18 years). Polygamy is legal, with men permitted to have four wives and unlimited number of temporary wives. Women are not permitted to travel or acquire a passport without their husband's written permission. A woman is not permitted to be in the company of a man who is not her husband or a male relative. Public activities are segregated. Women are not allowed to engage in sports in which they may be seen by men; or permitted to watch men's sports in which men's legs are not fully covered.

Although these laws were implemented with great brutality, women have always resisted. Recently in Iran there have been signs that women are increasingly rejecting subordinate lives ruled by the mullahs. Women have campaigned for inheritance rights equal to men's, and for more rights to custody of their children. Women keep modifying or enhancing their public dress in ways that press the limits of the hejab. More publications by or about women are appearing. Women are demanding they be allowed to participate in and view sports events. Many Iranian women want change.

Some analysts have said that the election of Mohammed Khatami [a reformist elected in 1997] to the position of President was due to the votes of women. Khatami's strongest distinction seems to be that he was not the

Image on previous page: A police officer detains a woman for not adhering to the strict Islamic dress code during a crackdown on "immoral" fashion in Tehran in 2007. (AP Photo/Hasan Sarbakhshian.)

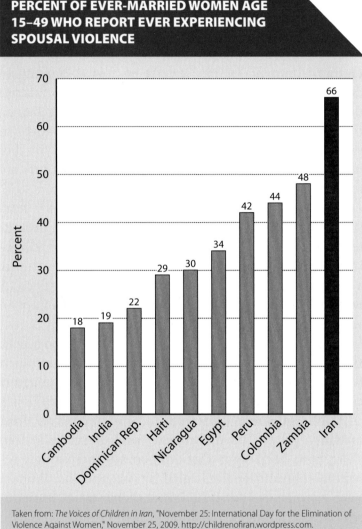

PERCENT OF EVER-MARRIED WOMEN AGE 15–49 WHO REPORT EVER EXPERIENCING SPOUSAL VIOLENCE

Taken from: *The Voices of Children in Iran*, "November 25: International Day for the Elimination of Violence Against Women," November 25, 2009. http://childrenofiran.wordpress.com.

hard-line government's favorite candidate. His election was no doubt a vote *against* the hard-liners. His upset election has garnered him the label of "moderate," and raised expectations of people inside and outside of Iran.

Khatami has been in office one year now. Is he a moderate? Has the status of women markedly improved in Iran since his election?

The Status of Women Twenty Years After the Revolution

There is a widely held view that Khatami supports the rights of women, but his statements and appointments don't validate that view. Prior to his election Khatami said, "One of the West's most serious mistakes was the emancipation of women, which led to the disintegration of families. Staying at home does not mean marginalization. Being a housewife does not prevent a woman from having a role in the destiny of her people. We should not think that social activity means working outside the home. Housekeeping is among one of the most important jobs."

Under Khatami's leadership the Supreme Council of the Cultural Revolution decided not to sign the United Nations Convention on the Elimination of All Forms of Discrimination Against Women (CEDAW), the most important international agreement on the rights of women. An international study comparing workforce conditions for women around the world ranked Iran 108th out of 110. In urban areas women make up only 9.5 percent of the workforce, and in rural areas the percent is 8.8. Even Khatami's advisor on women's affairs acknowledged that there is discrimination in employment and promotion against women in government offices: "Some officials are of the opinion that men have more of a role in running the family, so they favor the men."

Khatami has not called for an end to the most savage and sadistic punishment in the world—death by stoning. This form of torturous killing was initiated by fundamentalists when they came to power after the Islamic Revolution. Law specifies the size of the stones and the method of burying a person to be stoned. The purpose is to inflict great pain and suffering before death occurs.

> An international study comparing workforce conditions for women around the world ranked Iran 108th out of 110.

Since Khatami has been president at least seven people have been stoned to death in public, four of them women.

Khatami's advisor on women's affairs, Zahra Shoja'l, says she is an advocate of women's rights, but all within a fundamentalist defined Islamic context. She defends the restrictive and symbolically oppressive hejab, calling the chador [a full-body covering] "the superior national dress of the women of Iran."

Khatami's highly publicized woman appointment is Massoumeh Ebtekar, Vice-President for Environmental Protection. She has a long association with the fundamentalists: after the Islamic Revolution in 1979 she was spokesperson for the hostage takers who captured the U.S. embassy in Tehran. She does not favor loosening restrictions on women that would give them more personal freedom or stop the most barbaric institutionalized violence against women. She supports the law that requires women to get their husband's permission to travel. She justifies this law by saying, "Man is responsible for the financial affairs and safety of the family. Thus, a woman needs her husband's permission to make a trip. Otherwise problems will arise and lead to quarrels between them." She also defends stoning women to death by saying, "One should take psychological and legal affairs of the society into consideration as well. If the regular rules of family are broken, it would result in many complicated and grave consequences for all of the society."

Since Khatami was not the hard-line mullahs' favored candidate for presidency, his election has created factions within the Iranian government. A power struggle has ensued, but this is not an ideological fight between those loyal to religious fundamentalists and proponents of secular democracy. All sides, including Khatami, are committed to a theocracy based on velayat-e-faqeeh—the absolute supremacy of the mullahs.

> Women's public clothing continues to obsess the mullahs.

Draconian Laws Continue

After 1979, the measure of the success of the Islamic Revolution was the depth of the suppression of women's rights and activities. Now, nineteen years later, battles among factions within Iranian government are played out over women's rights, hejab and segregation.

Draconian laws and discrimination are not things of the past. Women's public clothing continues to obsess the mullahs. In the last year, the Martyr Ghodusi Judicial Center, a main branch of the judiciary, issued a stricter hejab, or dress code. The new guidelines call for prison terms from three months to one year or fines and up to 74 lashes with a whip for wearing "modish outfits, such as suits and skirt without a long overcoat on top." The regulations ban any mini or short-sleeved overcoat, and the wearing of any "depraved, showy and glittery object on hats, necklaces, earring, belts, bracelets, glasses, headbands, rings, neckscarfs and ties."

Women continue to be arrested for improper veiling. In November [1997], an Agence France Presse correspondent in Tehran witnessed approximately ten young women being arrested and placed into a patrol car for improper veiling or wearing clothing that did not conform to Islamic regulations. The women were wearing colorful headscarves and light make-up. In June Ayatollah Ali Khamenei told senior officials that it was time "to crack down on wanton behavior by women." By mid-August, 1,800 women and men had been arrested for "mal-veiling and lewd conduct." Most of the women were wearing makeup or in the company of young males who were not related to them. Women who fail to conform to the strict dress code are boarded on minibuses and taken to a center for fighting "social corruption."

Under fundamentalists' interpretation of Islamic texts, women are banned from being judges because they are not considered capable of making important decisions. One of the claims of moderation in Iran is the appointment of women as judges, but in actuality no women are allowed this rank. Judiciary Chief Yazdi recently made the issue clear in his Friday prayers sermon: "The women judges I mentioned hold positions in the judiciary, they receive salaries, they attend trials, they provide counsel, but they do not preside over trials and/or issue verdicts."

In the past year, women's groups campaigned for a bill that would give women the same inheritance rights as men, but Parliament overwhelmingly rejected the bill saying the proposal was contrary to Islamic law, which stipulates that a woman's share may only be one half that of a man's.

Women made a small gain by getting Parliament to pass a law that granted women some custody rights to children after a divorce, but only if the father was determined to be a drug addict, an alcoholic or "morally corrupt."

New laws strengthening gender apartheid and repression of women are not a thing of the past. During the last year Parliament and other religious leaders proposed a number of new laws or policies that will adversely effect the health, education, and well being of women and girl children in Iran.

New Laws Strengthening Apartheid

Temporary marriage, in which a man can marry a woman for a limited period of time, even one hour, in exchange for money, is permitted in Iran. Earlier this year, Ayatollah Haeri Shirazi, a prominent religious leader, called for a revival of this practice so clerical officials could have religious sanctioned sexual relationships with women. This practice is an approved form of sexual exploitation of women, and allows the regime to have an official network of prostitution.

In April, Parliament approved a new law requiring hospitals to segregate by sex all health care services. This will compromise the health care for women and girls because there are not enough trained women physicians and health care professionals to meet the needs of all the women and girls in Iran.

Another new law approved by Parliament imposes more restrictions on the photographs of women that can be published in newspapers and magazines. The Iranian state television announced on August 1 a decision by the Justice Department in Tehran to shut down a newspaper and put its proprietor on trial. One of the charges leveled against the publication, *Khaneh*, was that it had published "obscene" photographs of women playing football.

Parliamentary deputies submitted a plan to make girls' schools a "no-male zone," which will require all teachers and staff to be women. This requirement will make education for girls even more inaccessible and difficult. Official statistics recently released reveal that 90 percent of girls in rural districts drop out of school.

> Official statistics recently released reveal that 90 percent of girls in rural districts drop out of school.

More ominously, the Parliament also approved a law prohibiting the discussion of women's issues or rights outside the interpretation of Shari'a (Islamic law) established by the ruling mullahs. In a further effort to repress all discussion of women's rights, in mid-August, the Parliament passed a bill prohibiting the publication of material in the media that defended women's rights in a way that would create conflict between the genders. Advocates of women's rights are subject to imprisonment and lashing for violations.

In early July 1998, Mohsen Saidzadeh, a cleric, was arrested after writing articles that opposed these bills. He said that laws that deprive women of their rights are based on incorrect interpretations of the Koran. So freedom to criticize the government position on the rights of women does not exist even for fellow mullahs.

No Moderation

In some Western writings Khatami is said to have given new freedoms to the press, but the experience of publishers is contrary to that claim. In February, the newspaper *Jameah* started to publish articles critical of the government, color photographs of smiling women harvesting wheat, and an interview with a former prisoner. By June a court revoked their license. Also, police filed charges against *Zanan*, a monthly women's magazine, for "insulting" the police force by publishing an article on the problems women face with the authorities on Iranian beaches, which are segregated by sex.

> There was no improvement in human rights in Iran since [President Mohammed] Khatami took office.

Although Khatami is the President of Iran, he is not the Supreme Spiritual Leader, the most powerful position in Iran. The supreme leader, Ayatollah Ali Khamenei, controls the armed forces, the police, the security and intelligence services, radio and television, and the judicial system. The *velayat-e-fahiq* is a serious impediment to any reforms that may benefit women or society at large. Ayatollah Khamenei's opinion of women and their place in society is the same as his predecessor Ayatollah Khomeini's—women should be wives and mothers. Supreme Leader Ayatollah Ali Khamenei has publicly stated: "The real value of a woman is measured by how much she makes the family environment for her husband and children like a paradise." In July 1997 Ayatollah Khamenei said that the idea of women's equal participation in society was "negative, primitive and childish."

There is no moderation in Iran. Both the U.N. Special Rapportuer and the U.S. State Department found that there was no improvement in human rights in Iran since Khatami took office. The Iranian government engaged in summary executions, extrajudicial killings, disappearances and widespread use of torture. The hard-line mullahs will not lift the severe restrictions on women; in fact, they favor stronger gender apartheid. Khatami, although not aligned with the hard-liners, does not support the empowerment and emancipation of women from the *velayat-e-fahiq* or supreme rule of the mullahs. If the women in Iran want the rights and freedoms they deserve they will have to look elsewhere for change.

The Iranian Green Revolution Has Dangerous Similarities to 1979

Michael Singh

The following viewpoint argues that the Iranian Green Revolution of 2009–2010 has many parallels with the revolution of 1979 and with earlier revolutionary movements in Iran. The author notes, for example, that the Green Movement, like earlier movements, was brought about by a coalition of secular and religious forces. He argues that the success of past movements suggests that the Green Movement may triumph in the long term. However, even if it does overthrow the Iranian government, it may lead to instability, violence, and oppression as did the earlier revolution. Michael Singh is a fellow at the Washington Institute for Near East Policy.

SOURCE. Michael Singh, "Iranian Re-Revolution—How the Green Movement is Repeating Iranian History, *Foreign Affairs,* July 26, 2010. Reprinted by permission of Foreign Affairs, July 26, 2010. Copyright © 2010 by the Council on Foreign Relations, Inc. www.ForeignAffairs .com.

On June 10 [2010], when the Iranian opposition movement cancelled its planned commemoration of the anniversary of [Iranian president] Mahmoud Ahmadinejad's disputed reelection, commentators assumed that the Green Movement [the protest movement in Iran] was finally finished. For months, it had been criticized as lacking strong leadership and for being unable to seriously challenge Iran's entrenched regime.

Many Revolutions

But the history of political turmoil in twentieth-century Iran suggests that the movement may yet survive. After all, movements propelled by similar social currents have succeeded in dramatically changing Iran in the past.

Three periods of domestic political turbulence shook Iran in the last century—the Constitutional Revolution of 1905–1911, which for a time curbed royal power and led to the development of Iran's constitution; the Muhammed Mossadeq era of 1951–1953, which temporarily ousted Mohammad Reza Shah Pahlavi; and the 1979 Islamic Revolution, which replaced the monarchy with clerical rule.

> Although periods of upheaval tend to be remembered today as being driven by iconic leaders . . . , it is important not to forget how broad and longstanding the popular movements behind them actually were.

Each of these episodes was brought about by the confluence of three factors: increasing popular anger at the regime's corruption, a rupture between the ruling and clerical classes, and dissatisfaction with Iran's foreign relations. In each instance, two disparate camps—one secular and liberal, the other comprised of politically active (often young and mid-ranking) clergy—momentarily came together in opposition. Indeed, although periods of upheaval tend to be remembered today as being driven by iconic leaders such as Mossadeq, in the 1950s, and Ayatollah Ruhollah Khomeini, in 1979, it is important not to forget how broad and longstanding the popular movements behind them actually were.

In the early 1900s, for example, long-simmering outrage at the shah's tyrannical behavior and humiliating trade concessions to Russia and Great Britain boiled over when the director of customs (a Belgian national) began to enforce tariffs to pay off Russian loans. Intellectuals were joined by clerics, for whom the concessions were not only an affront to Islam but also a threat to the economic interests of religious endowments. The two camps came together to demand the ouster of the shah's prime minister and the establishment of a parliament. In the 1950s, nationalist revolutionaries campaigned to rid Iran of British control, citing the Anglo-Iranian Oil Company as a symbol of imperialist exploitation. Mossadeq spearheaded the movement but relied on Ayatollah Sayed Abol-Ghasem Kashani to rally an activist segment of the clergy. Kashani's example may have been an inspiration to Khomeini, who, in the 1960s and 1970s, brought together an extensive coalition, including secularists, clerics, youth, and others. In demanding an end to the monarchy, Khomeini and his associates seized on widespread disgust at the shah's coziness with Western powers and outrage over his oppressive and corrupt behavior. The coalition was galvanized by Mohammad Reza's land reforms, which threatened the financial base of clerics and other wealthy elites.

All three opposition movements took years to consolidate before becoming powerful enough to force change on the regime. The Constitutional Revolution, which is thought of as emerging around 1905, as protests broke out over tariffs, was in fact a continuation of events that began in 1891, with the campaign to overturn an exclusive tobacco concession the shah had granted to the British.

Similarly, Mossadeq's National Front achieved power in 1951, but this was after decades of discontent with a monarchy that had descended into disorder following World War II. The violence of this era was a longstanding family feud as well: before ousting Mohammad Reza in 1951, Mossadeq had been imprisoned by Mohammad Reza's father—Reza Shah—for, among other things, casting a dissenting vote in the parliament in 1925 against his coronation. The Islamic Revolution of 1979, moreover, had roots going back to 1960–1964, when riots against the shah swept the country and Ayatollah Khomeini and many other activists were exiled.

History Repeating Itself

Each period of turmoil was distinctive but was propelled by similar undercurrents. It is a peculiar irony that in today's campaign against Khomeini's political

During the riots following reformist presidential candidate Mir Hossein Mousavi's disputed loss in 2009, a supporter wears a green scarf, symbolizing the party's color. (**AP Photo.**)

heirs, the opposition movement is appealing to many of the same grievances Khomeini cited in his campaign against the shah. And indeed, the very same three factors that contributed to previous episodes of turbulence are converging again today. First, Ahmadinejad's apparent theft of the 2009 presidential election, and the regime's harsh repression of protests and other dissent preceding and following those elections, have fueled accusations of corruption and tyranny. This displeasure has been exacerbated by the popular perception that a privileged few—mainly elites in the Islamic Revolutionary Guard Corps—have benefited from Iran's resource wealth while average citizens have struggled. Second, the mounting international opprobrium directed at Tehran [Iran's capital] has created a sense that the regime's mismanagement of foreign relations is an embarrassment and harmful to Iran's interests. Finally, the clergy appear to be dissatisfied with the government (exemplified for now less by active opposition than by the dwindling clerical representation in government and the growing number of clergy who refrain from political activism on behalf of the regime), and some of the citizenry have even accused the regime of being "un-Islamic" for its policies of repression and torture.

This movement, too, is wide-ranging. It brings together not only reformists associated with Muhammad Khatami's more liberal government of the late 1990s, but also former conservative stalwarts, such as Mir Hussein Moussavi, the movement's leader. It also appears to be at least tacitly aligned with other hardliners, such as former President Ali Akbar Hashemi Rafsanjani, and with quiescent clergy, labor activists, students, and merchants who have grown unhappy with the regime's economic policies. All seek to curtail corruption, restore a greater measure of civil rights to Iranians, and establish a less dangerous, more productive relationship with the outside world.

Moreover, the Green Movement is built on discontent that predates the June 2009 elections: it is the same dissatisfaction that led to Khatami's landslide electoral victories in 1997 and 2001 and to the student protests between the late 1990s and today. Just as reform movements past were slow to build, today's cannot be declared over because of the Green Movement's apparent sluggishness. The mass protests following Ahmadinejad's election have shown that the regime has lost the affection of the majority of Iranians. So even as questions persist about the Green Movement's viability, the regime's viability is no clearer.

> "The mass protests following Ahmadinejad's election have shown that the regime has lost the affection of the majority of Iranians."

Cause for Caution

Yet if history gives cause for optimism regarding the opposition's prospects for success, it also gives cause for caution. Their primary goals achieved, the coalitions leading the past century's three reform movements quickly crumbled, riven by conflicting objectives and ideologies. After the Constitutionalists ousted the shah's prime minister and convened a parliament, they quickly found themselves pitted against clergy advocating an Islamic state. By 1911, Russian troops had shelled and disbanded the parliament, leading clerics had been executed, and Iran was controlled by the Russians in the north and the British in the south. Two years after coming to power, the coalition led by the National Front was similarly fractured, and communist partisans were the strongest force in the streets. A U.S.- and British-organized coup soon ousted Mossadeq. And finally, in the months after the Islamic republic was established, Khomeini's Iran plunged into bloody violence between competing factions. The regime likely only survived due to the unifying effect of the war with Iraq in 1980.

> The international community should . . . harbor no illusions that [the Green Movement] would inevitably lead to peace and democracy.

The international community should not worry that the Green Movement is doomed, but it should harbor no illusions that its success would inevitably lead to peace and democracy in the long term. Indeed, the United States and its allies should be considering not only how best to support the democratic aspirations of Iranians, but also how to prepare for the real possibility of instability in Iran should the opposition prevail.

The Iranian Green Revolution Is Not Similar to 1979

Danny Postel

The following viewpoint argues that the left wing of the 1979 Iranian Revolution was in part responsible for its own defeat. The author notes that the Marxist left in Iran saw liberal ideals of equality and feminism as part of an imperialist Western program. As a result, the left supported Ayatollah Khomeini when he rejected these egalitarian ideas, aiding Khomeini in establishing a totalitarian, reactionary government. The writer argues that the Green Revolution of 2009–2010 is, in contrast, committed to pluralism and freedom. He concludes that the Green Revolution has real emancipatory potential and deserves support. Danny Postel is communications coordinator of Interfaith Worker Justice, editor of *The Common Review*, and co-editor of *The People Reloaded: The Green Movement and the Struggle for Iran's Future.*

SOURCE. Danny Postel, "30 Years of the Islamic Revolution in Iran: Opening Remarks," *Platypus Review 20*, February 2010. http://platypus1917.org. Reproduced by permission.

T he central question, which I will approach indirectly, is whether the 1979 Islamic Revolution in Iran was a tragedy for the Left.

Not a Tragedy, but a Catastrophe

In the conventional narrative of the Iranian Left the answer to our question has long been, "Yes." The 1979 Revolution was a failure insofar as it was hijacked by one faction of a broader coalition that included the Iranian revolutionary Left. The faction in question was the Islamist or Khomeinite faction, which, once it gained control, proceeded to decimate, destroy, murder, imprison, and drive into exile its erstwhile comrades. There is a lot of truth to this leftist narrative, but it is only part of the story. It is largely self-exculpatory and elides the role the Iranian Left played in its own immolation. An account of this self-defeat can be found in Maziar Behrooz's book, *Rebels with a Cause: The Failure of the Left in Iran*, a salutary and, indeed, definitive reconsideration of the history of the pre-revolutionary Iranian Left.

> No, the 1979 Islamic Revolution in Iran was not a *tragedy* for the Left, for tragedies befall innocence.

As Maziar explains, the Iranian Left, or at least certain key factions of it, helped fashion the noose the Islamists ultimately hung them with. According to Behrooz, the Khomeinites were able to do this in large part because the Tudeh party, the Fadaiyan Majority, and many other Iranian Marxist parties, whatever their differences with the Islamists, shared with them a profound hostility toward liberalism. Like [Ayatollah Ruhollah] Khomeini's followers, dominant trends on the Iranian Left viewed democratic rights, civil liberties, and women's rights as no more than elements of what they described interchangeably as "western," "colonial," or "bourgeois" ideology.

On the basis of Behrooz's analysis of the critical failings of the Iranian Left, I would say we must revise the Iranian Left's usual answer to the question and answer it instead in the negative. No, the 1979 Islamic Revolution in Iran was not a *tragedy* for the Left, for tragedies befall innocence; they happen to people who have no idea of, and are not responsible for, the fate that awaits them.

This raises another question: Is it in fact a tragedy that the Stalinists and Maoists who made up the great majority of the left in Iran in the 1960s and 1970s did not take power? After all, virtually all Iranian leftists of the 1960s and 1970s were either Stalinist or Maoist. In light of this, I would argue that what followed in the wake of the 1979 Revolution was not so much a tragedy

Iranian director Shirin Neshat (center) and the cast of her film at the 2009 Venice Film Festival wear green in support of the Iranian opposition movement. **(AP Photo/Joel Ryan.)**

for the Iranian Marxist "Left" then in existence, as it was a tragedy for the project of the Left *per se*. For the genuinely leftist project of internationalism and human emancipation, the profoundly authoritarian, repressive, reactionary, and proto-fascist regime that emerged out of the Revolution and has ruled Iran ever since is certainly tragic but also, and more accurately, *catastrophic*. But what are the lessons to be learned?

There are both external and internal factors in the destruction of the Iranian Left. The external factors are obviously the brutality of the Islamists who took over and Iran's strategic position in the Cold War rivalry between the U.S. and USSR. These factors are certainly important, but Behrooz's book rightly zeroes in on the internal factors. Of these, he considers the Left's tunnel-vision anti-imperialism most essential. Khomeini's gang may have disdained professedly secular, rational socialists, but on the Left the argument went that, because they were anti-American and anti-imperialist, the Khomeinites were "objectively progressive."

> There was nothing progressive about Khomeini's anti-imperialism. It was authoritarian and regressive.

A Lethal Argument

We now know that the Left's was a demented, disfigured, ultimately catastrophic argument, one that had lethal consequences for those who propounded it. There was nothing progressive about Khomeini's anti-imperialism. It was authoritarian and regressive, as is [Iranian president Mahmoud] Ahmadinejad's anti-imperialism today. Whether Khomeini's rhetoric was truly anti-imperialist is open to debate—but to the extent it was, it amounted to no more than an anti-imperialism of fools.

What were some of the consequences of the Iranian Marxist Left's view that the anti-imperialist, anti-

American rhetoric of the Khomeinites was "objectively progressive"? As mentioned earlier, it led to a rejection of the demands for human rights advanced by feminists, democratic liberals, and nationalists. Rather than sympathizing with and advancing their demands, many on the Left in Iran in 1979 regarded feminism as a bourgeois colonial ideology. Because of this many Iranian Marxists sided with extreme reactionary forces within the new Islamic government as they repressed feminism, beating women and suppressing their demands. Similarly, when newspapers were shut down, many Iranian Marxists defended not their right to publish their views, but the regime's supposed responsibility to close them down! Here again the logic was the same: Liberal and nationalist newspapers were neo-colonial and bourgeois. Such actions, justified in the name of anti-imperialism, constituted a catastrophic turn down the dark alley of anti-liberalism. The Left mistakenly viewed liberalism as part of a toxic, global, colonial project rather than viewing it, as Marx himself did, as being necessary but insufficient—or, better, *insufficient but bloody necessary*—to the project of socialism and liberation.

The anti-liberal "radicalism" the Iranian Marxists shared with the Khomeinites was reactionary. But what can this teach us today, as we watch the protests in the streets of Tehran? After all, less than 24 hours ago [in February 2010], we witnessed the largest protests since the fall of the Shah. Clearly, we are again living in a historic moment, and so we should discuss some of the parallels and discontinuities between 1978–1979 and today, the most obvious similarity being that, once again, hundreds of thousands, if not millions, of Iranians have taken to the streets to voice their demands.

Where there has been some affinity between *Platypus*'s [the *Platypus Review*, where this viewpoint first appeared] perspective and my own is in our shared critique of the authoritarian Left, the myopic anti-imperialism of those like *MRzine*, the online organ of *Monthly Review* magazine, or an organization like international ANSWER [Act Now to Stop War and End Racism], which held a demonstration in solidarity with the Islamic Republic of Iran in June [2009] here in Chicago, defending Hugo Chavez and his position that the demonstrations in Iran are tools for imperial intervention, that the elections were wholly legitimate, and that Ahmadinejad is a revolutionary comrade that deserves the Left's support.

> I think there is a real danger in failing to recognize the emancipatory potential . . . in the Green Movement.

Pluralistic, Democratic Liberalism

Where my perspective diverges from *Platypus*'s is in our respective angles on what is happening in Iran today, particularly with respect to the Green or democratic movement that has developed in response to the June [2009] election results. As Chris Cutrone made clear already in his article in the August 2009 issue of the *Platypus Review*, he dismisses the Green Movement [the 2009–2010 protest movement] in Iran as still too . . . something. Actually I do not think Chris developed any definite criticism, but made only rhetorical gestures. So, I hope to hear an argument about where he stands now on the Green Movement in Iran. But from what I have heard so far from him, he shares the tunnel-vision anti-imperialism of the Left that supports Ahmadinejad and rejects the Green Movement. No doubt, he has reasons of his own for rejecting the Green Movement, but what he shares with the defenders of Ahmadinejad is a hostility to the pluralistic, democratic liberalism already articulated by the Green Movement. Though it is true that this movement remains somewhat inchoate, a work-in-progress, and is even now still forming its platform or agenda, the broad ideological outlines are clear.

I think there is a real danger in failing to recognize the emancipatory potential—not the fully articulated emancipatory program, granted, but the clear emancipatory promise and potential—in the Green Movement. It is a mistake to blind oneself to this promise or to reject it simply because it is articulated within the logic and framework of the Islamic Republic, or because it does not speak the anti-capitalist language of the Western Left and lacks a developed critique of neoliberalism. This latter point, which I take to be *Platypus's* position, represents a species of left imperialism. To decline to sign on and support the Green Movement because they do not speak the language of socialist revolution is to cram the complex and fluctuating on-the-ground reality in Iran today into the preconceived categories of the Western Left. Such an attempt to fit that movement into our agenda constitutes a disfigured left imperialism that fundamentally misunderstands Iran today.

CHAPTER 3

Personal Narratives

A British Diplomat's Eyewitness Account of the Revolution

Desmond Harney

In the following excerpts from his diary, a British diplomat discusses the day of the shah's departure from Iran—January 16, 1979—and the reaction. He notes the confusion about the exact moment of the shah's departure and the enthusiastic celebration in the streets that followed. He says that young people in particular were excited about the prospect of a new government and about the return of the Ayatollah Khomeini from his exile in Paris. The author expresses concern that the revolution may turn violent and his wishes that Prime Minister Shahpur Bakhtiar might have a chance to institute reforms. Desmond Harney lived in Iran for more than a decade as a diplomat and as a banker.

Photo on previous page: A woman sits by her son's grave in the Behesht-e Zahra cemetery in Tehran, where thousands of those killed in the revolution and the Iran-Iraq War are buried. (**Kaveh Kazemi/Getty Images.**)

SOURCE. Desmond Harney, "January 1979: 'The Shah Has Gone,'" *The Priest and the King: An Eyewitness Account of the Iranian Revolution*, I.B. Tauris & Co., 1999. Used by permission.

*T*uesday, *[January]* 16th *[1979]* (26 Dei 1357)
At eight minutes past one o'clock midday, the Shah left (*Shah raft*). On hearing it on the telephone from the Inter-Con came that sudden droop I recall having in the old days on hearing that a condemned man had been hanged at dawn in Wormwood Scrubs prison [in London].

The Shah Leaves

To the last it was a mixture of spoof, dignity and force. The press had been told to expect a press conference at the palace at 10 A.M. Only certain journalists were invited, and the unlucky ones fought like furies to get on the bus that was sent. Finally they left . . . not up the hill to the palace, but out to the airport. Anticipation grew. Was this it? Yes, it was. At the VIP lounge, cameramen, the Imperial Guard, Court dignitaries were drawn up.

> All over Iran the faithful believed they saw Khomeini's features on the surface of the moon.

They waited. Nothing happened. At 10:30 a spokesman calmly told them the departure was cancelled—till tomorrow perhaps. Consternation (in truth, I learned today that the Shah had been too overwrought to face the press). Then, shortly before 1 P.M., helicopters clattered and throbbed over my house in the bright sky, now partly clouded. In fact he left (together with the Queen) unobserved by the curious but with full honours—the PM [Prime Minister], the Minister of Court, Speakers of both Houses, etcetera all in attendance. By 2 P.M. it was on the news. Even up in chic Elahieh, cars started honking and tooting within minutes. The euphoria was on. Now what of the Old Man in Paris [the Ayatollah Khomeini, living in exile in Paris]? Can he be humoured to accept the great work [Prime Minister Shahpur] Bakhtiar has done in seeing the Shah off? Or will he release the seven avenging furies of popular revolution? A new chapter opens.

To herald all this, the latest 'supernatural' event occurred: yesterday all over Iran the faithful believed they saw Khomeini's features on the surface of the moon. And yet another earthquake struck Khorasan. Oh Iran, what a year of events! But to return to the popular reaction. Irresistible not to go out. Scenes of great excitement in the streets round us. Every car hooting rhythmically, flashing its lights. Crowds gathering at every junction: men grinning and giving the V-sign; girls in *chadors* [full-body coverings] singing and laughing; boys prancing about shouting at us to put on our lights or to slap pictures of Khomeini on the windscreen; groups shouting "Everyone is free now"; small demonstrations brandishing portraits of Khomeini aloft crying, "By the force of Khomeini, the Shah has fled."

We worked our way up through an old village district by then in a ferment of excitement and joy. Out onto Pahlavi Avenue where boys came up hammering on the bonnet advising us to put our lights out as ahead were "friends of the Shah": troops. Generally things became more subdued as we reached Tajrish Square. The reason was soon obvious: we had to go through a cordon of stern-looking troops—no flowers here—who were smashing windscreens with staves if one had one's lights on or a portrait of the Agha [i.e., Khomeini] on the car. So past a few truckloads where there was no joy or fervour. On to Niavaran and a turn round the palace, still bravely flying the pale blue imperial standard . . . but now empty. Unbelievable.

Then back into Khomeini country through the Chizar district. Lights on again, the honking renewed and we were back in the seedbed of this revolution—the alleys, bazaars and villages of old Tehran [Iranian's capital], alive with kids and teenagers jumping on garden walls, piling high on the roofs of vans, shouting their heads off, brandishing carnations and gladioli or portraits of the Agha (and occasionally one of scholarly, bespectacled [religious leader Sayyid] Shariatmadari) showering sweets on passing cars. Into the militant village itself which was smothered under slogans on the walls and plastered with that ominous black stencil of the victorious guerrilla brandishing his gun. Past my friend Goudarzi's mosque with about a hundred youths, boys, and girls in headscarves, shouting in unison and brandishing their fists: *Allah-u akbar, Khomeini rahbar* (God is great, Khomeini the Leader). Freedom had come; restraint had finally gone. Well, we'll see. The next few days will show. I myself doubt if Khomeini or his advisers will now relent one jot.

> I felt as I knew I would feel: that I could take no joy in their joy.

Finally as we reached home I felt as I knew I would feel: that I could take no joy in their joy. Are we faced with a victory, or even the beginning of a victory, of the great conspiracy against the West and of the resurgence of Islam? I have to give way to fears because one has to make personal decisions based on them: I fear Bakhtiar cannot last a week and will be swept aside. This worry was reinforced by a talk tonight to a clear-eyed German who has worked for many years running a farm in the countryside not far outside Isfahan. He has watched the events touch and then seize his own community. He remembers the day when a young mullah arrived in the village from Qom—not a complete stranger but a man who had distant antecedents there. Within days the subversion began: slogans on walls, talks to villagers, sermons by loudspeaker against the Shah and the government which recited all the simple themes we have learnt to know so well (and all of which we have a conscience about): the exploitation of Iran's oil, the corruption, the transfer of ill-gotten gains abroad, army brutality, the

corruption and obscenity of Western culture, etcetera, etcetera. Night after night, until 1 A.M., the loudspeaker blared out. And slowly the people turned.

Over weeks the village was politicised and my German friend—from being a popular benefactor and friend—found himself seen as an enemy. Yet he is one who had sympathised with them over the excesses and exactions they had had to undergo from a corrupt and arbitrary authority. He is one who was appalled by the clumsiness and coarseness of the huge American community in the vicinity which swamped the Iranians by its numbers and acted according to the worst canons of insensitive foreigners, even colonialists.

Thousands of Khomeini supporters demonstrated against the shah in front of a mosque in Tehran the day before the monarch left Iran. (**AP Photo.**)

The Morning After

Wednesday, 17th

The morning after. Fever abated, leaving a city plastered with pictures of the New Leader in abundant poses:

the famous posture squatting under the apple tree in his Paris garden, and endless variants of the stern, determined visage. The ruins of the revolution are the stumps of the once-proud statues, their pedestals now scrawled with slogans and covered in portraits, with a queer Islamic pennant or else a black banner stuck on the empty plinth. Youths were still scrambling over them and waving flags on high, but most were excitedly posing in front for memorial scrapbooks as they might in front of Nelson's Column [a monument in London]. Everywhere the crowds are kids or young roughneck teenagers, but behind are the bearded student marshals, now suddenly got up in olive-drab army jackets.

> After the Shah's departure . . . the joyous ones were rarely over twenty and often in their early teens.

The front of the university is seething revolution, with green flags, red flags, black flags, tens of hundreds of pictures of the Old Man, with an occasional hammer and sickle. Nowhere to be seen is any sign or mention of Bakhtiar (or the National Front for that matter)—not even to curse him. He might not exist. All is attributed to the Imam [a priest or Islamic leader]. The papers are full of that heart-rending, melancholy, but punctiliously correct departure of the Shah. Of his last look at the Elborz [Iranian mountain range] over his shoulder.

I remember so clearly on that exultant evening yesterday after the Shah's departure, that as we drove up the lanes of Maqsudbeg, the joyous ones were rarely over twenty and often in their early teens, and that on one corner stood an old wizened greybeard who, when I mouthed the question through the closed car window, 'Well, what's all this about?' merely shrugged in a baffled, hopeless kind of way and dolefully shook his head.

Speculation now centres on whether Khomeini is to return, and when. Some enter a new phase of wishful thinking that he won't from fear of being lost among the other ayatollahs. No such fate for such a magnificent and unbending campaigner! Of course he will come but only when he has swatted Bakhtiar aside . . . and the army too.

One of the best things of recent weeks has been the controversy at uptown parties. Everyone says they must not discuss politics—and then immediately does so. It is the stuff of life. Before, almost everyone was a grey area in this field—they said nothing on anything that mattered. The only ones whose views one really (presumably) knew were the courtiers and obvious Establishment figures—and even here one sometimes wondered. Now everyone is forced to show his true colours or—more likely—his medley and confusion of colours (at least in the circles we move in).

> How can Khomeini compromise? It is the conflict between the ghost of a monarchy . . . and an Islamic republic.

No Compromise

Thursday, 18th

[US president Jimmy] Carter now calls on Khomeini to 'give Bakhtiar a chance' and crassly asks him to desist from violence (he who has been calling, ostensibly at least, for an end to it). Sounds like pleading from weakness with the man who holds the trumps. But how can Khomeini compromise? It is the conflict between the ghost of a monarchy to which Bakhtiar is committed, and an Islamic republic which the masses are told they want. Only two things can restrain them: fear of the army's reaction; and pressure from the US which even Khomeini recognises he has to work with if he is not to fall under Russian influence. Surely the Saudis and others must be urging him to this? This must make him show his true colours.

In retrospect the mood today in town was like a hangover. One relived the night before, but without the fervour. People seemed dazed, desultory, uncertain. Even at dinner parties, Bakhtiar is simply not mentioned. Not even curiosity about the names or positions of his new ministers. Everyone assumes it is transitory—with hope that this good, brave and honest man is not afterwards branded a quisling [traitor].

Such contrary emotions on the Shah's departure. So many confess to weeping on hearing that he had left. Somehow, despite his aloofness, his arrogance, his manifest errors, the evils done in his name and—make no mistake—under his direction, this still youthful, fine-looking man who had been part and parcel of the lives of the great majority of Iranians since childhood, is felt for. People wanted to love him, but he didn't invite it. And now they see he was human and no mere police brute, into which role he is now being cast.

More stories of the 'revolutionary committees' (*komitehs*) forming in each bank, ministry, government agency, even embassies. Junior, disregarded clerks, holding their seniors to account—and being well briefed to do so. So far much of it seems only half-serious, part-imitative comic opera . . . until the bloodletting begins.

An Iranian Professor Describes Her Ordeal During the Revolution

Sattareh Farman Farmaian with Dona Munker

In the following viewpoint, a Persian woman discusses her experiences in the days following the Iranian Revolution. Her students had her arrested, accusing her of collaborating with the Western government of the shah. She notes that the students seemed to be using the chaos of the revolution to settle old scores and resentments. She reports that she was taken off to be interrogated by Ayatollah Khomeini; the students hoped she would be put to death. Sattareh Farman Farmaian was the founder and first director of the Tehran School of Social Work and is the author of numerous books, including *Prostitution Problems in the City of Tehran*. She was released from prison unharmed but, fearing for her life, she left her country for the United States.

SOURCE. Sattareh Farman Farmaian with Dona Munker, "Part Four: Earthquake: 15: The Party of the Wind," *Daughter of Persia: A Woman's Journey From Her Father's Harem Through the Islamic Revolution*, Doubleday, 1993. Used by permission.

The next morning, cheerful at the prospect of returning to work and hence in an optimistic frame of mind, I rose well before dawn. Half a foot of snow had fallen during the night, covering the leafless branches of the apple trees and the tin roots of the villagers' houses. I hurried out to start my car so that it could warm up. As I dressed, I listened for the ordinary dawn sounds of the village, the bustle of farmers taking their cows for milking at the dairy stable. But the dirt lane outside my wall was filled only with snow-muffled silence.

Uneasy, I dressed as quickly as I could, swallowing a cup of coffee as I put on the black clothes I was still wearing in mourning for my mother. Hurriedly I threw on a light black coat and kerchief to keep me warm until I reached the office, grabbed my handbag, and went outside to my car. It was bitterly cold, but as I threaded along the dark lane I was relieved to see a few farmers trudging just ahead. The main road had been cleared, and this, too, seemed a good omen. As the sun rose I passed the giant looted army base of Lashkarak, where three unsmiling revolutionaries in assorted garb and different-colored helmets stood before the gate. They waved their rifles and machine guns at me in excitement, shaking their fists solemnly and shouting, "Allahu akbar!" My hands tensed on the steering wheel. But at least, I thought, to judge from this the warring factions were working together now instead of killing each other. So far, Ayatollah Khomeini's call for order seemed to be a success.

In the village of Niavaran, where the royal family had lived, I drove by the palace. Even at this hour there was a crowd in front of it, but the tall Imperial Guardsmen who had always stood there were gone. Nervously, I speeded up a little to avoid the crowd. I wondered what would be done with the palace—perhaps it would become a museum, like Golestan, the palace of the Qajars. Reaching the city's northern outskirts, I was encouraged to see people standing on the sidewalks waiting for buses, while

Iranians are executed by Islamic firing squads on March 11, 1979, at Tehran's Qasr Prison. **(AP Photo.)**

others looked as though they were walking to work, maneuvering around the still-standing barricades and the hulks of burned cars and army equipment. I felt better. Perhaps things would be calm enough by summer for our women and children who were abroad to return, and then we could be a real family again.

I arrived shortly after seven and left the car in the parking lot by the side of the main building; Hossein or one of the other drivers would park it when they came to work later. I glanced around to see who else was there. Normally Zabi, our several gardeners, and the other servants started working at seven, too—Zabi considered it his job to carry my briefcase, books, and camera to my office for me—but I saw no one. Indeed, the parking lot, garden, and buildings seemed deserted, almost eerily quiet.

> 'There are students inside with guns, waiting to kill you.'

Suddenly, as I started up the stairs, Zabi dashed out of a side entrance and ran toward me. His face was ashen, and I wondered what was the matter. "Good morning, Zabi," I called cheerfully. "Is everything all right?"

He hurried close to me. There was terror in his eyes. Barely moving his lips, he whispered, "No, Khanom. There are students inside with guns, waiting to kill you."

I stared. Had he suddenly taken leave of his senses? "But why would any students be here before eight?" I asked stupidly. "Classes don't start till then."

"Please, Khanom," he begged, "you must leave. They are serious. I don't want them to see me talking to you."

I hesitated. "Where are these students?"

"In front of the library. They are blocking the way to your office."

Still I could not believe him. "Are you sure they are social work students? *Our* students?"

"Oh, yes, Khanom. One of them used to go with you in the Land Rover to wave the white flag. There are three others as well. They say they are going to kill you."

I paused to collect my thoughts. I could think only that this was a student notion of a prank that I didn't think was funny. "Well," I said, "take my things from the car and I'll go and talk to them."

With Zabi faltering behind me, I marched up the stairs to the glass doors and turned into the corridor that led to the library and my office. Sure enough, four boys in jackets and tieless shirts were standing there. One was a junior named Isadi who had often come with me to pick up victims of the fighting; another was a skinny, pockmarked senior named Ashari. There was also a sophomore, Kharmandar, and another second-year boy whose name I couldn't remember. All four carried semi-automatic machine guns. Two or three other students clustered behind them looking frightened; they did not appear to be with them. I saw no other servants besides Zabi, and realized that they must all be hiding. Zabi had shown great courage in slipping out to warn me. Well, I thought, if these boys were trying to give Khanom a scare, they were going to be disappointed. I wasn't going to scream and drop dead just because somebody pointed a gun at me.

I walked forward. Ashari, who was evidently their leader, quickly stepped to the center of the corridor to bar my way. The other three, still grasping their weapons, clasped hands behind him to form a barricade. "What's this all about?" I demanded coldly.

"You wouldn't send me to Bombay last year," the one whose name I didn't know said in a sulky voice. Isadi chimed in loudly but uncertainly: "You were always asking the mother of the Queen to our commencement ceremonies. You are an imperialist." Kharmandar's complaint was that he had failed his sociology exam the previous semester and had had to spend the summer studying to retake it.

> 'You are with the oppressors. You were trained in the imperialist country of America. You are one of them.'

"Ayatollah Khomeini says that the time has come for all the dispossessed to throw out their oppressors," Ashari said. "You are with the oppressors. You were trained in the imperialist country of America. You are one of them, and this school has been serving the imperialists and the CIA. We are taking you to Ayatollah Khomeini to ask him to execute you."

When I stared at him, too astonished to react at once, he frowned heavily. "We are going to ask Ayatollah Khomeini to execute you," he repeated. "He is going to kill you."

Suddenly I realized that I had better do something quickly. There was a tiny room opposite the library that we used as our information office. It had a telephone. Swiftly, without giving the students time to think, I dashed across the hall and, darting into the room, slammed the door and locked it. Since the government was gone, calling the police was probably useless. I decided to call Ahmad Mossadegh, who was a friend of Premier Bazargan.

Hastily, I dialed my cousin's office. To my relief, he was there. Assuring me that the students could not arrest me without a warrant, Ahmad urged me to call Ayatollah Mahmoud Taleqani. Taleqani, he said, was one of Khomeini's closest advisers, and was a reasonable man. Along with telephone numbers for Taleqani's office and home, Ahmad gave me Bazargan's office number, where he said Taleqani might also be found.

> These students weren't religious zealots or even committed radicals—they were what the oil boom years and the disappointments that followed had produced: immature, bitter, resentful young men.

Hastily thanking him, I hung up and dialed the office number at once. A sympathetic assistant said that the Ayatollah was not in. However, he confirmed that the students could not arrest me without a warrant. All arrest warrants were issued only from revolutionary headquarters, and they were only for the apprehension of the Shah's high generals and for former officials, SAVAK men, and notorious police informers. "Make them show you their warrant," he urged me. "They must have one in their hands to arrest you."

Gratefully I hung up, about to go outside again. Then it occurred to me that the students might cut the telephone wires. I always went to Jaby's for lunch on Saturday; I had better let her know what was happening. I picked up the phone again. The line had gone dead.

Furious, I put back the receiver. What was going on? I vaguely remembered that the boy who talked about going to Bombay had wanted to go there for an International Planned Parenthood Federation training course—the IPPF itself had turned him down because he couldn't speak English. Kharmandar was angry because I had refused to override his professor's decision to flunk him. Apparently, in the spirit of the moment, they were tagging along with the other two for revenge. But why were Ashari and Isadi trying to make me out to be an "oppressor"? Isadi had always cheerfully volunteered to go along to gather the dead and wounded. Ashari was a dull, depressed youth who had been imprisoned by SAVAK for two years. Zamani and my director of academic affairs, who were on the screening committee, had reported that he was too self-absorbed and introverted to make a good social worker, but his grades had been acceptable and I had felt that anyone who had been a victim of SAVAK should be given a chance; besides, prison must have made his emotional problems worse, and perhaps studying social work would help him. I had not only admitted him, but given him financial support. He wouldn't be standing there now, I thought contemptuously, if I hadn't felt sorry for him.

I suppressed my emotions and tried to think. I was fairly certain that these students weren't religious zealots or even committed radicals—they were what the oil boom years and the disappointments that followed had produced: immature, bitter, resentful young men who felt that society had failed to give them what it had promised, and whose version of Marxist theory was that if somebody owned what they wanted, he should give it to them instead of keeping it for himself. With the School grown so big, it had been hard to keep such boys out. There were many young men like Ashari now, who felt entitled to a reward for having chosen the winning side. No one would take their accusations seriously, but they had guns, and it was just possible, I realized, that they were doing this at the behest of someone in the new regime. I had no one now who could tell me who that might be. All my family's and the School's connections were gone, swept away with the old order. Of everyone I knew, only Ahmad might be able to find out, and now I couldn't reach him. I would just have to go back and ask the students calmly for their warrant. Displaying impatience or trying to defend myself would only increase the danger to me and any others in the hallway.

I unlocked the door and stepped outside again. Zabi had vanished in terror. Ashari was looking disgruntled at my temporary escape, which had undercut his moment of victory. Speaking in as neutral a voice as I could command, I asked him if they had a proper warrant.

"We have a warrant," said Isadi, and grinned, patting his gun. "Here it is."

Taken aback, I wondered what to do next. More students were filing into the building from the other end of the corridor, and so were teachers and field supervisors. They were smiling and talking as they arrived, as happy to be returning to work as I had been. God only knew, I thought, what Ashari and the others might do with those guns. It would be best to go along with them, and insist on the legalities later. But if enough people arrived in the meantime, perhaps they would be intimidated into reconsidering what might simply be a vicious but unplanned and impulsive act of malice.

"Well, then," I said, stalling, "what are you going to do?"

"We are going to take you to Ayatollah Khomeini," Ashari repeated sullenly. "He will execute you." I thought briefly of trying to talk him out of it, then gave up the idea. He would only take it as an insult and get angrier. There was no way I could reason with boys like this.

We stood about awkwardly for a minute or two. More people were arriving, men and women who had been with me for years, some since the beginning—teachers, supervisors, clerical staff. I didn't see Esther, but Zamani's wife, who was on my research faculty, had just walked in with a field supervisor who had often come on our Friday hikes. I waited for someone else to start talking to the students, for someone to ask why they were arresting me. All my graduates had been taught how to defuse tense situations and knew what to say to make people less angry and defensive. Each moment that Ashari hesitated would make him less likely to persist.

But minutes seemed to pass and no one spoke. I stared at the faces behind the students in surprise, then in growing alarm. I didn't expect anyone to defy the students or attempt to disarm them, but when someone was talking about killing me, was no one even going to ask what I had done?

Just then three more people came in through the front entrance. I glanced around. One was not a social worker but a part-time professor of research who taught at several other colleges in the city. But the other two, who served as directors of two of our welfare centers in South Tehran, were my own graduates—conscientious, hardworking men who had been among my first students, and whom I had known well for twenty years. They would certainly understand how to talk to Ashari and his gang.

The students looked over my shoulder and saw them, too. Suddenly galvanized into action, they began pushing excitedly toward them to surround them, exclaiming that they worked for an exploiter of the people and must meet the same fate as she. Shocked, the research professor tried to explain that he had merely come to give his weekly lecture. The two directors looked first at the guns, then at me. A kind of recognition seemed to dawn in their eyes. They glanced at me in fright, then at the students who surrounded us. Then one of them, with an imploring expression, looked at Ashari, pressed his hands flat against his breast, and gave me a sidelong look that said more clearly than any speech, "Surely you do not think that I am an oppressor, like her? I am on *your*

> They and I had shared bread and salt. Now not one was raising a word in my defense.

side." The other director nodded in agreement with the unspoken words. Thirty people behind Ashari watched in silence, their faces impassive.

Suddenly Ashari turned around, unsmiling but triumphant. "I have important news!" he shouted. "The Islamic revolutionary fighters have won. Now it is we who will run this place! We are taking the director and these members of her staff to Ayatollah Khomeini to be executed!"

There was a pause of no more than a heartbeat. Then somebody called out, "Allahu akbar!" At once, other voices joined in. "Allahu akbar," they cried, "God is great—hurrah!"

In disbelief I looked first at one face, then another. It was as if we were all in a bad movie together and everything was happening in slow motion. I felt as though someone had driven a knife between my ribs, but as yet there was only shock, not pain. I could understand that they might all be afraid to protest, but why, I wondered dully, were they cheering? I saw staff members and graduates I had taught fifteen or twenty years ago. They were people whom I had coaxed and comforted through fieldwork, had sent abroad to study and found good jobs, whose families I had helped in emergencies, who had consulted me on everything from financial problems to the choice of a marriage partner. Twenty years passed before my eyes, twenty years of hard, unending labor on behalf of our profession and of these people, for whom I had felt responsible. They and I had shared bread and salt. Now not one was raising a word in my defense.

I looked at Ashari again. His eyes looked back at me with feral distrust. The idea that such a creature was planning to run the School of Social Work was so disgusting that I felt almost physically ill. Without trying to disguise the contempt I felt, I said, "Well, if that is what you are going to do, then let us go and do it."

We went outside to the parking lot where one of the Land Rovers was waiting. The students had selected a driver named Zarabadi. He was a man of about forty, whom I had hired when he told me that his wife and children were sick for lack of proper food, and who often came now to tell me how well his family was doing. I was sorry that the students were forcing him to drive.

> His joy sounded completely authentic. He was sincerely glad that I was about to die.

The students bundled us into the big vehicle, I in the second row between the professor of research and Kharmandar, and the two directors in the back seat with the fourth student, who held his gun on us to make sure we didn't try to jump out and run away. Isadi and Ashari, handing Zarabadi a large white handkerchief to wave, climbed in front and we set off southward toward Shahreza Avenue. The road was cluttered with burned and scattered wreckage, sandbags, and hunks of cement.

Zarabadi drove slowly and carefully, avoiding the rubble, while Ashari stuck his arm out the window, waving his own handkerchief importantly. At the intersections farther into town, traffic was being directed not by the regular blue-uniformed city police but by pairs of bearded or stubble-faced young men in the odd assortment of paramilitary gear we had been seeing ever since the army's surrender. A few wore Arab headdress, and once, when we stopped near a couple, I heard them talking to each other in Arabic. I wondered in passing why Arabs were directing traffic in Tehran. Where were the ordinary police? At all these intersections, the students leaned out and veiled triumphantly, "Allahu akbar! We are taking traitors to Ayatollah Khomeini to be executed!" The men outside did not smile, but nodded and solemnly shook their fists in congratulations.

When we reached Shahreza Avenue, Zarabadi suddenly rolled down his window, too. "Hey," he yelled, laughing, "look what I have—I am taking four traitors to Ayatollah Khomeini! These people will soon be shot!" The guard waved him on. Still laughing, Zarabadi turned left onto Shahreza. I could hardly believe my ears. His joy sounded completely authentic. He was sincerely glad that I was about to die.

The Ayatollah Khomeini Discusses His Vision of Iran

Ayatollah Khomeini, interviewed by Oriana Fallaci

In the following viewpoint, an Italian journalist interviews Ayatollah Khomeini eight months after the Iranian Revolution. She asks him about his ideas of freedom and democracy and suggests that his regime is dictatorial and fascist. In particular, she points to the silencing of liberal media outlets and to the executions of prostitutes and homosexuals. Khomeini replies that Islam cannot be fascist, that his government must root out the enemies who wish to destroy it, and that liberals are enemies of the state who sympathize with the former shah. He says that adulterers, prostitutes, and homosexuals cause moral corruption, which may destroy the state, and must be stopped before they cause damage. Oriana Fallaci was an author, and political interviewer. Muslim cleric Ayatollah Khomeini ruled Iran as Supreme Leader from 1979 until his death in 1989.

SOURCE. Oriana Fallaci, Interview with Ayatollah Khomeini in *Interviews with History and Conversations with Power*, Rizzoli Publications, 2011. Used by permission of Rizzoli Publications.

riana Fallaci: Imam Khomeini, the entire country is in your hands. Every decision you make is an order. So there are many in your country who say that in Iran there is no freedom, that the revolution did not bring freedom.

Ayatollah Ruhollah Khomeini: Iran is not in my hands. Iran is in the hands of the people, because it was the people who handed the country over to the person who is their servant, and who wants only what is good for them. You saw very well how after the death of [Ayatollah Mahmoud] Taleghani [in September 1979] millions of persons went into the streets without the threat of violence. This shows that there is freedom. It also shows that the people only follow men of God. And this is freedom.

> It is unjust and inhuman to call me a dictator.

Forgive me if I insist, Imam Khomeini. I meant that today, in Iran, you raise fear, and many people call you a dictator. The new dictator, the new boss. The new master. How do you comment on that? Does it sadden you or don't you care?

On the one hand I'm sorry to hear that. Yes, it hurts me, because it is unjust and inhuman to call me a dictator. On the other hand, I couldn't care less, because I know that wickedness is a part of human nature, and such wickedness comes from our enemies. Considering the road that we have chosen, a road that is opposed to the superpowers, it is normal that the servants of foreign interests treat me with their poison, and hurl all kinds of calumnies against me. Nor do I have any illusions that those countries which are accustomed to plundering and looting us will stand by silently and idly. Oh, the mercenaries of the shah say lots of things—even that Khomeini ordered the breasts of women to be cut off. Tell me, since you are here, did you have any evidence that Khomeini could commit such a monstrous act, that he would cut off the breasts of women?

No. I did not, Imam. But you frighten people, as I said. And even this mob which calls your name is frightening. What do you feel, hearing them calling out like this, day and night, knowing that they are there, all of them there sitting for hours, being shoved about, suffering, just to see you for a moment and to sing your praises?

I enjoy it. I enjoy hearing and seeing them. Because they are the same ones who rose up to throw out the internal and external enemies. Because their applause is the continuation of the cry with which the usurper was thrown out. It is good that they continue to be agitated, because the enemies have not disappeared. Until the country has settled down, the people must remain fired up, ready to march and attack again. In addition, this is love, an intelligent love. It is impossible not to enjoy it.

Love or fanaticism, Imam? It seems to me that this is fanaticism, and of the most dangerous kind. I mean, fascist fanaticism.

No, it is neither fascism nor fanaticism. I repeat, they yell like this because they love me, and they love me because they feel that I care for them, that I act for their good. That is, to apply the commandments of Islam. Islam is justice. Dictatorship is the greatest sin in the religion of Islam. Fascism and Islamism are absolutely incompatible. Fascism arises in the West, not among people of Islamic culture.

Perhaps we don't understand each other or the meaning of the word fascism, Imam. By fascism I mean a popular phenomenon, the kind we had in Italy when the crowds cheered Mussolini, as here they cheer you, and they obeyed him as they obey you now.

No, Because our masses are Moslems, educated by the clergy—that is, by men who preach spirituality and goodness. Fascism would be possible here only if the shah were to return or if communism would win and wipe us out. Cheering, for me, means to love freedom and democracy.

Okay, then, let's talk about freedom and democracy, Imam. And let's do it like this. In one of your first speeches at Qum, you said that the new Islamic government would guarantee freedom of thought and of expression for everyone, including Communists and ethnic minorities. But this promise was not kept, and now you define Communists as "sons of Satan" and the leaders of the rebelling ethnic minorities as the "evil of the earth."

First you affirm something, and then you expect me to explain your statement. You even presume that I should permit the plots of those who want to bring the country to anarchy and corruption—as though freedom of thought and of expression were the freedom to plot and to corrupt. Therefore, in answer to your question, I say: For more than five months I tolerated, we tolerated, those who did not think as we do. They were free, absolutely free, to do whatever they wanted. They fully enjoyed the freedom that was granted to them. I even invited the Communists to have a dialogue with us. But, in response, they burned the wheat harvest, they burned the urns of the electoral offices, and they reacted to our offer for a dialogue with rifles and arms. In fact, they were the ones who stirred up the problem of the Kurds [an ethnic minority in Iran]. Thus, we understood that they were taking advantage of our tolerance to sabotage us, that they did not want freedom but the license to subvert, and we decided to stop them. And when we discovered that, urged on by the former regime and foreign forces, they were seeking our destruction with other plots and other means, we shut them up to avoid further problems.

For example, by closing the newspapers of the opposition. In that speech at Qum you also said that to be modern means to form men who have the right to choose and to criticize. But the liberal newspaper Ayandegan *was shut down. And so were all the leftist newspapers.*

The newspaper *Ayandegan* was part of the plot I mentioned. It had relations with the Zionists; it got ideas from them to do harm to the country. The same goes for all the newspapers that the attorney general of the revolution judged subversive, and then closed; newspapers which, through a phony opposition, tried to restore the old regime and to serve foreign interests. We shut them up because we knew who they were, and what they were after. And this is not contrary to freedom. This is done everywhere.

> Let us say that freedom is when you can choose your own ideas and think about them when you please.

No, Imam, it is not. In any event, how can you call those who fought against the shah, who were persecuted, arrested and tortured by him, as being "nostalgic for the shah"? How can you call them enemies, how can you deny them a place and the right to exist, those leftists who fought and suffered so much?

None of them fought or suffered. If anything, they took advantage of the anguish of the people who fought and suffered. You are not very well informed. A good part of the left which you refer to was abroad during the imperial regime, and came back only after the people had overthrown the shah. Another group was here, it is true, hidden in their houses. It was only after the people had shed their blood that these leftists came out to take advantage of that blood. But until now nothing has happened to limit their freedom.

At this point, Imam, I must ask you what you mean by freedom.

Freedom—it is not easy to define this concept. Let us say that freedom is when you can choose your own ideas and think about them when you please, without being forced to think something else. Let's say that freedom is to live where you want, and to do the work that you like.

To think, not to express or to make your thoughts concrete? And by democracy, what do you mean, Imam? I'm asking this question with much curiosity because in the [March 1979] referendum on whether there was to be a republic or a monarchy, you prohibited the expression "Islamic Democratic Republic." You banned the word "democratic," saying, "Not a word more, not a word less." As a result, the people who believe in you use the term "democracy" as though it were a dirty word. What's wrong with this noun, which seems so beautiful to us in the West?

To begin with, the word "Islam" does not need adjectives such as "democratic." It is sad for us to add another word near the word "Islam," which is perfect. Besides, this "democracy," which you love so much and that you consider so valuable, does not have a precise meaning. Aristotle's democracy is one thing, the democracy of the capitalists is still another. We cannot afford to have such an ambiguous concept placed in our constitution.

Let's talk about the 500 executions that took place in Iran after the victory. Do you approve of the summary way in which these trials are taking place, without lawyers, without the chance for an appeal?

Evidently in the West you ignore, or you pretend to ignore, who was being executed. They were persons who participated in massacres in the streets and the squares, or persons who ordered those massacres, or persons who burned down homes, who tortured, who cut off the arms and legs of those who were being interrogated. What should we have done with them, granted pardons and let them go free? The right to defend themselves, and to respond to accusations—we gave them those chances. But once their guilt was demonstrated, what need was there, or is there, for an appeal? Write the contrary if you want, the pen is in your hand. My people do not ask your questions. And I will even go further: Had we not executed those criminals, the revenge of the people would have gone beyond control. Every functionary employee of the regime would have been executed. And the dead would have numbered far more than 500. They would have been in the thousands.

> "What brings corruption to an entire country and its people must be pulled up like the weeds that infest a field of wheat."

All right, but I did not necessarily mean the torturers and the Savak [the shah's secret police] killers, Imam. I meant those who were executed and had nothing to do with the regime, the people who are still being shot today for adultery or prostitution or homosexuality. Is it right to shoot the poor prostitute, or a woman who is unfaithful to her husband, or a man who loves another man?

If your finger suffers from gangrene, what do you do? Do you let the whole hand, and then the body, become filled with gangrene, or do you cut the finger off? What brings corruption to an entire country and its people must be pulled up like the weeds that infest a field of wheat. I know there are societies where women are permitted to give themselves to satisfy the desire of men who are not their husbands, and where men are permitted to give themselves to satisfy other men's desires. But the society that we want to build does not permit such things. In Islam, we want to implement a policy to purify society, and in order to achieve this aim we must punish those who bring evil to our youth. Don't you do the same? When a thief is a thief, don't you throw him in jail? In many countries, don't you even execute murderers? Don't you use that system because, if they were to remain free and alive, they would contaminate others and spread their stain of wickedness?

Americans Captured in Iran Discuss Their Experiences as Hostages

Rocky Sickmann and William Gallegos, interviewed by Rita Cosby

The following viewpoint is excerpted from the transcript of a televised interview with two former Iranian hostages, twenty-five years after their release. The two discuss the harsh conditions of their imprisonment. They say how they were repeatedly threatened with death, sometimes held in isolation, and generally subject to cruelty and abuse. They also discuss the difficulty of freeing hostages in foreign countries, and their frustration that Iran has not been held accountable for the hostage taking. Rita Cosby is a television news anchor and correspondent, radio host, and author. US Marines Rocky Sickmann and William Gallegos were stationed at the US embassy in Iran when they were held hostage for 444 days by the government of Ayatollah Khomeini.

SOURCE. Rocky Sickmann and William Gallegos, interviewed by Rita Cosby, "Twenty-Five Years Later, Iranian Hostages Speak," MSNBC, January 23, 2006. Used by permission.

Friday marked the 25th anniversary of the release of the last Americans held hostage in Iran. The hostage situation tormented Americans for 444 days after Iranian militants raided the U.S. embassy in Tehran [Iran's capital].

Sixty-eight people were seized on November 4, 1979. Some were released. But 52 were held until January 20, 1981. The former U.S. hostages gathered Thursday [January 19, 2006] in Washington, D.C., to mark the anniversary of the end of their horrible ordeal.

Two of these former 52 hostages, Rocky Sickmann and also William Gallegos, joined Rita Cosby on [MSNBC news show] *Live and Direct* to recall their painful ordeals. Former NYPD [New York Police Department] hostage negotiator Wally Zeins also joined to discuss hostage situations.

> You don't forget the things that they put you through, the mock-firing squads, the Russian roulette, being tied to a chair for 30 days not allowed to speak, being locked in a room for 400 days.

Rita Cosby: Let me start with you, Rocky. You know, it's been 25 years. But do you still have nightmares? It must just stay with you for the rest of your life, what you went through?

Rocky Sickmann: It really does, Rita, and probably not so much nightmares. But there are things, just like as you were showing clips of fellow comrades that are being taken and have been taken—and you see those masked individuals with rifles—I remember it as it was like yesterday.

If you've been through a trauma like a car accident, you never forget that car accident. Being held hostage for 444 days, you don't forget the things that they put you through, the mock-firing squads, the Russian roulette, being tied to a chair for 30 days not allowed to speak, being locked in a room for 400 days. Those are traumatic experiences that you just can't zap from your brain.

A hostage is paraded in front of a mob outside the US embassy in November 1979. **(AP Photo.)**

I cannot even imagine. . . . You know, William, let's go back to that fateful day, November 4, 1979. What went through your mind when the students raided the embassy? Did you have any idea that you and those others would be taken hostage?

William Gallegos: No, I didn't at that time. I thought we'd be able to fight them off. It didn't seem to work out that way.

You know, when you look back, is there something different you could have done? I know you were given orders, "Don't shoot." Do you think it would have been worse, had you shot?

Gallegos: I think it would have been worse had we shot that day. I think, if we had done that and the marines started shooting the people that are coming over the fences or in through the doors, we possibly would have all been killed at that time.

You know, Rocky, at one point, they take you and the others into a room, and they stripped you. Tell us, what did they say, what did they do at that point?

Sickmann: Yes, at the very beginning, Rita, you know, everybody was interrogated. And they put us into rooms and brought political prisoners in, because what they wanted from us is to have us state derogatory statements against our government, [saying that the US government wanted] the Shah to return and [saying] how bad our government was.

So they brought political prisoners in. They, you know, told us what the Shah had supposedly done to them. And then, weeks later, after they had shown us one specific film, where it was shot from the rooftop, individuals in the courtyard, stripped nude, told to turn, and they were shot in the back of the head.

Well, February 1980, we were in our room. And we had made Uno cards out of paper. And we're sitting there playing Uno at 2:00 in the morning, because you have to create your own living condition within that room.

And all of a sudden, at 2:00 in the morning, the door burst open. In the room come two individuals masked with rifles drawn. And they pull us out of the room and against the wall, down [in] the basement in the embassy, where [there were] other fellow hostages.

Right away, you're thinking the United States government's coming to rescue us. They know about it, and they're getting ready to shoot us, because they told us, "If anybody comes to try to rescue you, as the hostages, we will shoot you."

> 'If anybody comes to try to rescue you, as the hostages, we will shoot you.'

And all of a sudden, as you sit there against the wall, hands against the wall, I mean, my body was releasing fluids everywhere. I mean, you're scared. I mean, anybody that tells you that they weren't scared, I'd have to question what the heck was going on in their mind.

But you're sitting there thinking of your past. I mean, your mind plays all kinds of games when you're taken from, you know, your life. And all of a sudden, they grab me and threw me into a room. And three individuals come in. And they locked and loaded and said, "Undress."

And right away, your mind goes back to those movies that they had shown you about these political prisoners. And all of a sudden, here I am, buck naked, and they said, "Turn around." And after they told me to turn around, I thought there's the movie, three bullets to the back of the head. And then it never obviously happened.

But again, when you're held hostage in a foreign country and you have no control, you have no idea what's going on, it was a very traumatic situation that you just don't ever forget.

Rocky, you were there in 1979. It's astounding. You kept that journal, and you were able to sneak it out. It's incredible. I read the story that you taped it on your leg. On April 26, 1980, Rocky, you wrote in your journal—and I think this quote is so powerful—"They blindfolded us and they took us down back of the embassy. We rode in the van for nine hours, blindfolded, handcuffed, and not being able to talk to anyone." And then they moved you around quite a bit after [the US military rescue attempt failed]. How terrified were you when they loaded you in that van the first time, Rocky?

Sickmann: I have a very vivid memory of that, Rita. That evening, you could tell something was happening at the American embassy that day. You could hear things. You could never see them, but you could hear people running around. Cars were driving up and down.

And all of a sudden, about 10:00, I think it was, that night, they came into the room and said, "You must go to the restroom." Well, Rita, you couldn't leave the room unless you knocked on the door and put a piece of paper underneath the door. And then they blindfolded you and took you to the restroom.

> That's the disgrace that . . . it's like someone had raped me of 444 days of freedom and they've never been [held] accountable.

Well, you know, they all of a sudden blindfolded us, took us to the restroom, came back, and all of our things were, like, in bags. And they said, "Gather your stuff. We must leave."

And all of a sudden, they blindfolded us, handcuffed us, and then took us down the back of the embassy, put us in the back of the vehicle. Jerry was handcuffed, I believe, to my right. I was handcuffed to him. Billy was to my left, handcuffed to him. Billy was handcuffed to the suburban.

They took a picture of us. And all of a sudden, they threw a blanket over top of us. And, again, here you are. It's like April. I've been there for some time. And you're sitting there thinking, "You know what? This isn't good."

And sure enough, they drove us that night. We had no idea what had happened. Drove us to another destination. And, I mean, Rita, if you had to go to the bathroom that night, there was no stopping at the pit stop, you know, and be able to go up and go to the clean bathroom. You had to go on yourself.

I mean, that's the disgrace that, for 444 days, this country that did this to us, it's like someone had raped me of 444 days of freedom and they've never been [held] accountable. It was a difficult time. We remained at the spot that they took us to the next morning. They then kept us in this safe house.

We went outside that afternoon. They put us back into the vehicle that night, and they drove us south of this location, supposedly to Shiraz.

Incredible. You know, Rocky, it is incredible when I hear the stories of what you and William went through.

Iranian Exiles Discuss Life After Leaving Iran

Mehrdad Haghighi and Lily, interviewed by Zohreh T. Sullivan

The following viewpoint contains excerpts from interviews with two Iranians who fled their country because of their religion. Both are members of the Baha'i faith, an Iranian monotheistic religion targeted for persecution by the post-revolutionary Islamic government. One exile, Mehrdad Haghighi, discusses the atrocities committed by the Iranian government, his own escape, and the hardship he faced establishing a new life in the United States. The other exile, Lily, talks about her longing for her home in Iran, and her hopes that she will return someday. Zohreh T. Sullivan is an emeritus professor of English and African studies at the University of Illinois at Urbana-Champaign.

SOURCE. Zohreh T. Sullivan, "Mehrdad Haghighi, From Here: Reconstructing Migration and Exile," *Exiled Memories: Stories of Iranian Diaspora*. Used by permission of Temple University Press. Copyright © 2001 by Temple University. All rights reserved.

Zohreh T. Sullivan: [In the following section, Mehrdad Haghighi] describes his flight into exile. This is also a segment that shows the difficulty of separating the story of "here" with the story of "there." The memory of revolution persists in erupting through the boundaries of present experience.

Escape and Hardship

Mehrdad Haghighi: I was on the last plane that left Shiraz [a city in Iran] for the [Persian] Gulf States and landed at Qattar. After waiting for twelve hours at the airport with my one-year-old son and my wife, we left for Pakistan. I was detained there for ten days. Although my passport identified me as a journalist, they gave me a hard time at the airport. They even tore up my shoulder pads in their body search. This was all in General Zia's time [General Muhammad Zia-ul-Haq, president of Pakistan in the late 1970s and 1980s]. But when I arrived in London, my identification as a journalist worked to my advantage, so that I was given a visa to the United States with no trouble.

When I arrived in the United States, I had only $800 left of the $1,200 that I was able to bring out of Iran. One of my dear friends took me to his house that night, and the next day at 7:00 A.M., I was at work in his printing press. Four days later, my wife, who is a physical therapist, found a position in a downtown Los Angeles hospital. We rented a house that was very dirty. I took off my shoes to walk up the six flights of stairs with my luggage. When I returned, my shoes were gone. We had no furniture, so I used a cardboard box as my desk. The only money I spent was to buy a radio to prevent me from going insane. Soon we got our work permits and after a hundred days, we got our green cards. I used to put my son in his pram and go around distributing flyers for supermarkets at $3.50 an hour. People warned us that we couldn't take it and that we would want to return to Iran in three months. Instead, we got our green cards. Exactly eight months after our arrival I was able to rent a nice house in which we are still living. For the first time, we enjoyed sleeping in real beds and eating breakfast at a table. Eleven months after arriving here I bought a car.

I had left all I owned in Shiraz, and after my departure the building in which I had my office was burned down because on the ground floor was a liquor store. I had about eight thousand volumes of books, newspapers, and magazines that I had collected for several years. These were all lost in the fire. My house was plundered. My father was in the house, and he lost his sight. Then he was jailed. The administrator of the mosque near our house took a towel and visited Ayatollah Dastgheib. He said to the Ayatollah, "Either release this man or cut off his head and place it in this towel I have in my hand." Because this man was much respected, he was able to get my father out and to get an exit permit for my father, who then came here for treatment. After my father's departure, they put this same administrator in jail, accusing him of being a Baha'i. My father, still in treatment and unwell, flew back to Iran. Ayatollah Mahalati asked him why he had returned. He said, "This man endangered his life and freedom for me. I will not let him suffer for that. He stood as a guarantor for me. I am here. Let him go." They released the man and put my father in jail. One night Ayatollah Mahalati went to him and said, "You have twelve hours to get out of the country, and I beg you to leave." He gave my father a ticket, and my father went to Spain.

> The point of a revolution is to guide and free the people, not to take away their lives and freedom.

The Purpose of the Revolution

Six of my friends were hanged. The point is not what religion you have. The point of a revolution is to guide and free the people, not to take away their lives and freedom. I saw some awful things. I witnessed the little son of my friend getting up early one morning and saying, "I dreamt that they have killed my father." In fact his father had been put to death in prison that very morning. When they went to visit him in jail, they gave them the body to take away. What legacy have these people left?

Many were put to death. The purpose of a revolution should be to teach a better way of life, not to eliminate the opposition. I can understand penalizing the opposition in a way that is instructive. In India, for instance, a man who had killed the father of a family with small children was sentenced to work for eighteen years on the victim's farm until his children grew up. Wouldn't that be of more benefit to society than simply eliminating people? My problem with religion occurs when it becomes a force for suppression. It was not only the killing of the Baha'is that affected me. I had a friend whose sister was a Mojahid [a Muslim fighter]. Why was he executed? I had a friend who was Zoroastrian [an ancient religion based on the teachings of Zoroaster]. Why was he executed? What caused a revolution within me was the description of how some of these friends were subjected to physical and mental torture. When I finally read the last testaments written by these people and saw photographs of their bodies, I broke down. I don't understand why, when a woman was guilty, the jailers needed to wring the neck of that woman's small child as well. What makes someone stretch the limits of barbarism to the extent of first pulling out a person's tongue while he is still alive and then executing him?

As you know, I am a journalist, and I believe in

> I don't understand why, when a woman was guilty, the jailers needed to wring the neck of that woman's small child as well.

documenting things. I have kept copies of the last wills and testaments of these people and the letters of my friends and the photos of atrocities. There is a letter written by the sister of Sheedokht Baghaa who was in Evin Prison. When she asked her sister what she would like in jail, the response was, "Bring me contraceptive pills so that I won't carry the fetus of these men." There was so much rape of women in the jails. We need a museum that will hold these documents, so that the world will someday understand the extent of these atrocities.

However, here I am in California, fourteen hundred miles away from Iran. And my voice from this distance resembles the story of the man in a lunatic asylum. Someone went up to him and said, "You don't seem crazy, so why did you end up here?" The man replied, "I believed the whole world was crazy and the whole world considered me mad. Since they were in the majority, they won."

Lily's Story

Zohreh T. Sullivan: Earlier . . . Lily spoke of her childhood in Iran, her marriage, and her work for children's literature and for the literacy campaign. [In this segment], she responds to my question about exile.

> What do I miss? Most of all I miss our people, and I miss our mountains.

Lily: Six months after my husband left, I got my passport and the official permit to leave the country. I left our wonderful house with two suitcases of autumn clothing—as if I were to return in three weeks. We were planning to return and work in Iran. Our children were planning to return and work there. Three months after our arrival in the United States, the real persecution of Baha'is started. We were told to stay out and not go back.

Do you consider yourself an emigré or an exile? What do you miss most?

Definitely I think of myself as an exile. Wherever I am, I am an outsider. I wish to be in Iran and I miss Iran. Here, I work. I like what I do. Though I live in the West, whatever I do in education is mostly for the third world because that is my way of feeling nearer to Iran. If for a minute I thought that I would never go back, I would die. I understand very well that if ever we did go back, Iran would not welcome us.

What do I miss? Most of all I miss our people, and I miss our mountains. Being Iranian is so many things. It is language, our books, culture, music, the way people look, the eyes, the eye contact. You know, I lived in Thailand for four years and for a part of that time lots of Iranians used to come to Thailand. They were mostly Hezbollahi people [supporters of Ayatollah Khomeini], with whom I didn't want to associate, but I would stand many a time in the corner and just watch them because they were young Iranians. Maybe it's very sentimental. Most probably it is. But I have this fear—I am always afraid now to become a chauvinist. I love Iranians just because they are Iranians. And that's not right. I prefer to think of myself as an internationalist. I have just finished a book on that—a book for children called *The World Is My Home, and Mankind My Family*. A person who writes that cannot be a chauvinist. Right? But Iranians and Iran have a special spot in my heart, and I cannot do anything about it.

GLOSSARY

Mahmoud Ahmadinejad
Conservative president of Iran beginning in 2005. His re-election in 2009 was widely disputed and resulted in the Green Revolution of 2009–2010.

Baha'i
Monotheistic religion established in nineteenth-century Persia (present-day Iran) emphasizing the spiritual unity of human-kind. There are about 300,000 Baha'i in Iran, making it that country's largest minority religion. The Baha'i have long faced persecution by the Muslim majority in Iran.

Shahpur Bakhtiar
Political figure associated with the National Front, a party opposed to the shah. His appointment to prime minister by the shah in 1978 was intended to mollify the revolutionary forces. After the return of Ayatollah Khomeini to Iran, Bakhtiar's government was rejected by the masses, and he was forced to leave the country for France. He was assassinated in 1991 by agents of the Iranian government.

Green Revolution
Protest movement in Iran following the disputed 2009 presidential election, in which conservative candidate Mahmoud Ahmadinejad was declared the victor. The protests were repressed in 2010.

Ayatollah Seyed Ali Hoseyni Khāmene'i
President of Iran from 1981 to 1989 and Supreme Leader since June 1989, following the death of Ayatollah Khomeini.

Ayatollah Khomeini (Ruhollah Khomeini)
Religious leader and politician who opposed the shah and led the Iranian Revolution of 1979. Following the revolution, he was Supreme Leader of Iran until his death in 1989.

Mohammad Mossadegh
Democratically elected prime minister of Iran from 1951 to 1953. Mossadegh was a member of the liberal National Front party, which he created. He nationalized the Iranian oil indus-try, angering Western governments. He was overthrown in a coup d'état backed by the US Central Intelligence Agency.

mullah	A Muslim religious leader.
National Front	Democratic, liberal party founded by Mohammad Mossadegh in the late 1940s. The National Front continues as an opposition party.
Reza Shah Pahlavi	Ruler of Iran from 1925 until 1941. He was forced to abdicate in favor of his son, Mohammad Reza Shah Pahlavi, often known simply as the shah.
Persia	Another name for Iran.
SAVAK	Secret police under the shah, operating from 1957 to 1979. SAVAK was established with the help of the CIA and Israel's Mossad. It was known for torturing and executing opponents of the shah's regime.
the shah (Mohammad Reza Shah Pahlavi)	Monarch of Iran from 1941 until his overthrow in the revolution of 1979. He was known for secularizing and modernizing Iran and for his repression of dissent, especially through the SAVAK, the Iranian secret police force.
Shari'a	Islamic law.
Shiite Muslims	Second largest Muslim denomination in the world. Shi'ite Muslims are a majority in Iran, and Iran's government is a Shiite theocracy.
Sunni Muslims	Largest Muslim denomination in the world. Sunni Muslims are the majority in the Middle East, except Iran.
Tehran	The capital city of Iran.
White Revolution	Reform program launched by the shah in 1963 to modernize Iran and shore up support for his dynasty. It focused on land reform which was designed to appeal to the peasantry and also extended the vote to women. Many of the reforms were not popular. The White Revolution radicalized Ayatollah Khomeini, who began to speak out against the shah and was eventually instrumental in overthrowing his regime.

CHRONOLOGY

1941 September 16: Mohammad Reza Pahlavi, the shah, replaces his deposed father and becomes the constitutional monarch of Iran.

1953 August: The United States and Great Britain arrange the overthrow of popularly elected Iranian prime minister Mohammad Mossadegh. The constitutional monarchy is undermined and the shah effectively becomes an authoritarian ruler.

1962 October–November: Ayatollah Ruhollah Khomeini opposes the shah's efforts to allow women and non-Muslims to vote.

1963 January: The shah announces plans for a "White Revolution" to reform and Westernize Iran.

June: Khomeini denounces the shah. He is arrested, and massive demonstrations break out. In suppressing the demonstrations, security forces kill hundreds.

1964 November: Khomeini is exiled from Iran.

1970 Khomeini publishes his book *Islamic Government* from exile; it is smuggled into Iran and widely distributed.

1978 January: A government media campaign against Khomeini sparks antigovernment demonstrations.

September 8: On "Black Friday," the shah declares martial law. Peaceful demonstrators are attacked and more than eighty are killed, including three women.

October 3: Khomeini is forced out of Iraq; he travels to Paris.

1979   January 3: Shahpur Bakhtiar is appointed by the shah as a compromise prime minister.

January 16: The shah leaves Iran.

February 1: Khomeini returns to Iran.

February 11: Bakhtiar's government collapses; Khomeini assumes control of a revolutionary Iran.

April 1: A national referendum establishes an Islamic republic in Iran.

November 4: Islamic students occupy the US embassy in Tehran and take sixty-six Americans hostage.

1980   April 25: A US military mission to rescue the Iranian hostages fails.

July 27: The shah dies of cancer in exile in Egypt.

September 22: Iraq invades Iran, touching off the Iran-Iraq War.

1981   January 20: Iran frees the American hostages.

1982   June 21: Though Iraqi forces have been pushed out of Iran, Khomeini refuses a cease-fire and orders Iranian troops to invade Iraq.

1988   August 20: The Iran-Iraq war ends.

1989   June 3: Ayatollah Khomeini dies.

FOR FURTHER READING

Books

Slater Bakhtavar, *Iran: The Green Movement*. Irving, TX: Parsa Enterprises, 2009.

David Farber, *Taken Hostage: The Iran Hostage Crisis and America's First Encounter with Radical Islam*. Princeton, NJ: Princeton University Press, 2005.

Brendan January, *The Iranian Revolution*. Minneapolis: Twenty-First Century Books, 2008.

Nikki R. Keddie, *Modern Iran: Roots and Results of Revolution*, Updated Edition. New Haven, CT: Yale University Press, 2006.

Stephen Kinzer, *All the Shah's Men: An American Coup and the Roots of Middle East Terror*. Hoboken, NJ: John Wiley & Sons, 2003.

Charles Kurzman, *The Unthinkable Revolution in Iran*. Cambridge, MA: Harvard University Press, 2004.

Baqer Moin, *Khomeini: Life of the Ayatollah*. New York: I.B. Tauris & Co. Ltd, 2009.

Arzoo Osanloo, *The Politics of Women's Rights in Iran*. Princeton, NJ: Princeton University Press, 2009.

Amir Taheri, *The Persian Night: Iran Under the Khomeinist Revolution*. New York: Encounter Books, 2008.

Robin B. Wright, *The Last Great Revolution: Turmoil and Transformation in Iran*. New York: Random House, 2001.

Periodicals

Aljazeera: Frost Over the World, "Remembering the Islamic Revolution," February 21, 2010. http://english.aljazeera.net/programmes/frostovertheworld.

Shaul Bakhash, "The Iranian Revolution," *New York Review of Books*, June 26, 1980. www.nybooks.com.

BBC News, "Iranian Revolution: Your Memories," February 9, 2009. http://news.bbc.co.uk.

BBC News, "Women's Rights Under Iran's Revolution," February 12, 2009. http://news.bbc.co.uk.

BBC On This Day, "1979: Shah of Iran Flees Into Exile," January 16, 1979. http://news.bbc.co.uk/onthisday.

David Burnett, "How I Got that Shot of Ayatollah Khomeini," *Slate*, November 11, 2009. www.slate.com.

William J. Daugherty, "Jimmy Carter and the 1979 Decision to Admit the Shah Into the United States," University of North Carolina at Chapel Hill, January 3, 2003. www.unc.edu/depts /diplomat.

Economist, "Iran and the American Hostage Crisis: Those Were the Days," May 11, 2006. www.economist.com.

GQ, "444 Days in the Dark: An Oral History of the Hostage Crisis," November 3, 2009. www.gq.com.

Roya Hakakian, "Egypt Through the Lens of Iran's 1979 Revolution," *Time*, February 13, 2011. www.time.com.

John Kifner, "The World; The Angry Decade of the Ayatollah," *New York Times*, June 11, 1989. www.nytimes.com.

Shane M. "A Different Iranian Revolution," *New York Times*, June 18, 2009. www.nytimes.com.

Hooman Majd, "Think Again: Iran's Green Movement Is a Civil Rights Movement, Not a Revolution," *Foreign Policy*, January 6, 2010. www.foreignpolicy.com.

Azadeh Moaveni, "Most Fundamentalist," *New York Times*, May 7, 2009. www.nytimes.com.

Haroon Moghul, "4 Reasons Why Egypt's Revolution Is Not Islamic," *Religion Dispatches*, January 28, 2011. www .religiondispatches.org.

NPR Online, "Remembering Iran's 1979 Islamic Revolution," August 17, 2009. www.npr.org.

Dominic Sandbrook, "After the Revolution," *New Statesman*, June 16, 2009. www.newstatesman.com.

Tehran Times, "Mubarak and the Shah of Iran, Two Clone Dictators," February 16, 2011. www.tehrantimes.com.

Time, "Man of the Year: An Interview with Khomeini," January 7, 1980. www.time.com.

James Zumwait, "Setback in Women's Rights Is Khomeini's Trademark," *Human Events*, July 27, 2009. www.humanevents.com.

Websites

The Choices Program: Iran Through the Looking Glass: History, Reform, and Revolution (www.choices.edu/resources/scholars_iran.php). This website is part of the Choices Program, a national educational initiative based at Brown University's Watson Institute for International Studies. The page includes an extensive topically organized list of links to videos of scholars discussing the causes, events, and results of the Islamic Revolution of 1979.

Foreign Policy (www.foreignpolicy.com). The website of a leading foreign policy magazine, this resource includes extensive coverage of Middle East issues, including the Iranian Revolution of 1979, the Iranian Green Revolution, and the Middle East revolutions of 2011.

US Department of State: Iran (www.state.gov/p/nea/ci/ir). This US government site includes press releases, major reports, statistics, archival materials, and links to other resources.

INDEX

A

ABC (TV network), 75, 76

Abolghassem, Kachani Sayed, 62

Abourezk, James, 79

Adultery, 163–164

Afghanistan, 39, 43, 66

Agence France Presse, 117

Ahmadinejad, Mahmoud, 123, 126–127, 132, 134

Algar, Hamid, 92–93

Algerian Revolution, 107–108

Amini, Ali, 101, 109

Amnesty International, 71

Andrew, Christopher M., 5

Anglo-Iranian Oil Company, 33, 124

ANSWER (Act Now to Stop War and End Racism), 134

Anti-Americanism, 6, 75

Anti-shah movement, 12–16, *15*

Apartheid, 111–114

Arabs, 72, 104

Aristotle, 162

Associated Press, 91

Atlanta Constitution (newspaper), 79

Ayandegan (newspaper), 161

B

Baha'ism, 5, 100, 174–176

Bakhtiar, Shapur
Iran National Front and, 16

Khomeini regime and, 138–144

shah's regime collapse and, 20, 22–23, 24n1

Ball, George, 79

Baloochis, 72

Bani-Sadr, Abolhassan, 39, 43–44, 54, 83, 84

Bashir, Mohammed, 23

Bazargan, Mehdi, 16, 26, 35, 150

BBC, 6, 63

Behrooz, Maziar, 130–132

Bird, Kai, 89

Black Friday (Sept. 8, 1978), 14, 61, 99

Book banning, 89

Borujerdi, Horayn, 4

British embassy in Iran, 29–37, *34*

British Petroleum, 67

Brodsky, Matthew RJ, 6

Brown, L. Dean, 77

Brzezinski, Zbigniew, 39, 42

Bush, George H.W., 40

Bush, George W., 68

C

Cambodia, 114t

Cambridge History of Islam (Lewis), 91–92

Cancer, 65, 70

Capitalism, 162

Carter, Jimmy
Bakhtiar, Shapur, and, 143

185

cartoon, 19

diplomatic relations with Iran, 40,
58–59

embargo on Iran, 40, 45

hostage crisis and, 39–40

human rights and, 66

shah's ruler and, 64

CBS (TV network), 79

Censorship, 14

Chador, 52, *55*, 116, *136*, 139

Chase Manhattan Bank, 84

Chavez, Hugo, 134

Chicago Tribune, 81

Child custody, 111

Chile, 72

Christian Science Monitor (newspaper), 52

Christianity, 77, 100, 105

Christopher, Warren, 42

CIA, 20, 63–64, 84, 149

Clark, Ramsey, 79

Clothing

chador, 52, *55*, 116, *136*, 139

hejjab (Islamic veil), 50–54, *55*, 111,
112, 113, 116, 117

immodest dress, 51, 52, 111

punishments for violations, 113, 117

Cold War, 83, 132

Colombia, 114t

Communism, 58–59, 61, 80, 99, 127, 160
See also "Islamist Marxism;" Marxism;
Non-Marxist socialism

Constitutional monarchy, 12, 57

Cosby, Rita, 165–171

Cronkite, Walter, 75

Cutrone, Chris, 134

Cyrus the Great, 13, 100

D

Dalyell, Thomas, 32

Dastgheib, Ali Mohammad, 174

De Villemarest, Pierre, 63

Demonstrations

anti-shah movement, 12–16, *15*

Black Friday and, 14, 99

Khomeini, Ruhollah, and, 5, 12, 14, 65,
139

martial law and, 61

US demonstrations, 134

US embassy in Iran, *41*

women's clothing restrictions and,
51–52, *53*

Diplomatic immunity, 5

Dominican Republic, 114t

Drooz, Daniel B., 79

Du Berrier, Hillaire, 61, 64, 66

E

Ebtekar, Massoumeh, 116

Education, 57, 72, 119, 145–156, 176–177

Egypt, 44–45, 65, 114t

Embargo on Iran, 33, 40–41, 43, 45

Emergency Committee for the Defense of
Democracy and Human Rights, 96

Ettalaat (newspaper), 18

European Economic Community, 43

Executions, 65–66, 120–121, *147*, 163–
164, 168

Exxon, 67

F

Factional Politics in Post-Khomeini Iran
(Moslem), 4

Falk, Richard, 89, 90, 96

Fallaci, Oriana, 157–164

Fanon, Franz, 92, 108

Farah, Empress, *21*, 60

Fascism, 159–160

Fisher, Roger, 82

Flag burning, *41*

Ford, Gerald, 58

Foreign Affairs (magazine), 91

Foucault, Michel, 96, 98–109

Franco, Francisco, 100

Freedom Movement, 14–16

French Resistance, 63

G

Gallegos, William, 165–171

Gender Apartheid, 111–114

Ghotbzadeh, Sadegh, 43–44, 83

Goliniewski, Michael, 62

Griffiths, Eldon, 30

Guatemala, 72

Gurvitch, Georges, 108

H

Haghighi, Mehrdad, 172–176

Haiti, 114t

Hansen, George, 79

Hardy, Roger, 6

Harney, Desmond, 137–144

Harper's Magazine, 95

Harvard University, 69, 82

Health care segregation, 118–119

Hejjab (Islamic veil), 50–54, *53*, *55*, *112*, 116, 117

Hezbollah, 177

Homosexuality, 162–163

Hooglund, Eric, 11–16

Hosain, Imam, 16

Hostage crisis of November 1979
Bani-Sadr, Abolhassan, and, 43–44
Ebtekar, Massoumeh, and, 116
failed rescue, 38–49
Khomeini, Ruhollah, and, 6, 44
media reportage, 75, 81–82
personal stories, 165–171
photographs, *41*, *167*

House of Commons (UK), 27–37

Hudson Institute, 80

Hughes, Donna M., 110–121

Human rights, 24, 65–66, 93, 110–121

Human Rights Committee, 24

Hurd, Douglas, 30, 32, 34–37

Hussein, Saddam, 6

Huyser, Robert, 64–66

I

Imams, 104, 105, 108, 142

Imperial Guard, 138

India, 114t, 175

Intercontinental Hotel (Tehran), 19

International Planned Parenthood Federation, 150–151

Iran, government
Islamic Republic, 6, 25–28, 90, 116
Khomeini rise to power, 5, 65–67, 124, 138–144
martial law, 14, 61
monarchy, 6, 12, 23, 57
political spirituality, 98–109
shah regime collapse, 5–6, 12–13, 17–24, 26, 44–45, 123, 144

Iran-Iraq war, 6–7

Iran National Front, 14–16, 99, 125, 127, 142

Iranian Green Revolution, 122–135
Iraq, 5–7, 12, 40, 62, 68, 78
"Islamic Marxism," 22, 59
Islamic republic, 6, 25–28, 90, 116
Islamic Revolutionary Guard, 126
Israel, 5, 58, 68

J

Jameah (newspaper), 120
Jews and Judaism, 77, 90, 100
Jihad, 95
Johnson, Lyndon, 47
Jordan, 77
Judges, 117–118

K

Kalb, Marvin, 79–80
Kashani, Sayed Abol-Shasem, 124
Kashif al-Asrar (*Secrets Revealed*;
  Khomeini), 4
Kedourie, Elie, 77
Keith, Leslie, 50–54
Kennedy, Edward (Ted), 40, 59, 66
Kerr, Malcolm, 95
Khamenei, Ali, 117, 120
Khaneh (newspaper), 119
Khatami, Mohammed, 113–116, 120,
  126–127
Khomeini, Ruhollah
  anti-shah movement and, 12–15
  arrest, 5, 12
  Bakhtiar, Shapur, and, 22, 138–144
  biography, 4–7
  death, 7
  exile, 5, 12, 60, 62, 101–102, 125, 138,
    142
  freedom and, 158, 160–161, 162
  Hezbollah and, 177
  hostage crisis of November 1979 and,
    39, 44
  intelligence source for USSR, 62
  interview with reporter, 157–164
  Iran-Iraq war and, 6–7
  Islamic Republic creation, 25–28, 90
  Marxism and, 130
  media and, 5, 13–14, 65, 77, 81
  photographs, *10*, *103*
  Rabbi, Amir Hossein, and, 64–65
  rise to power, 5, 65–67, 124, 138–139
  shah departure and, 22, 58
  shrine, 7
  student uprisings and, 145–156
  United States as "great satan" and, 46, 91
  Western-style modernization and, 28
  women's rights and, 51–52, 62, 111, 120
  writings, 4, 90–93
Khomeini and Israel (Souresrafil), 5
Khuzestan, 26
Kissinger, Henry, 58, 67
Koran, 102, 119
Kraft, Joseph, 85–86
Kurds, 72, 160

L

Lahidji, Abdel Karim, 24
Land reform, 5, 62, 124
Language, 72, 77, 155
Laqueur, Walter, 76
Lashing, 113, 117, 119
Last Shah of Iran (Nahavandi), 58
Lebanon, 77, 99
Lehrer, Jim, 83
  See also Macneil/Lehrer Report
Lewis, Bernard, 77, 92

Lewis, Flora, 76–77

Literacy, 57, 70, 176–177

Live and Direct (TV news program), 166

London School of Economics, 77

Lorenz, Dominique, 62

Los Angeles Times, 80

M

MacNeil, Robert, 83

MacNeil/Lehrer Report (TV news program), 78, 80, 82–83

Mahalati, Ayatollah, 174

Majles (Iranian parliament), 12–13

Marriage, 111, 113, 118

Martial law, 14, 61

Martyr Ghodusi Judicial Center, 117

Martyrdom, 81, *82*, 85, 104, 108

Marxism, 20, 66, 79, 130–133, 151
See also Communism; "Islamist Marxism," Non-Marxist socialism

Massignon, Louis, 108

Media
cartoons, 19
censorship, 14, 89, 119, 120, 161
correct interpretation of Iranian Revolution, 88–97
demonization of Iranian Revolution, 74–84
human rights and, 66, 120
Iranian Green Revolution and, 133–135
Khomeini, Ruhollah, and, 5, 13–14, 65
misinformation about Iran, 60–63
response to shah's departure, 18

Menges, Constantine, 80

Middle East Institute, 77

Mitrokhin, Vasili, 5

Moghadam, Nasser, 99

Mohammed (Muhammad), prophet, 76, 104

Monarchy, 6, 12, 23, 57

Monthly Review (magazine), 1347

Montreal Gazette (newspaper), 25–28

Moslem, Mehdi, 4

Mossadegh, Mohammad, 12, 33, 123–125, 127, 150

Moussavi, Mir Hussein, 126

MRzine (online magazine), 134

Mullahs, 6, 20, 108, 111, 113, 116–117, 121, 140

N

Nahavandi, Houchang, 58, 63

Napoleon, 78

Nation (magazine), 89, 93–94

Neshat, Shirin, *131*

New Republic (magazine), 76, 80

New world order, 68

New York Police Department (NYPD), 166

New York Times, 76

Newsom, David Dunlop, 46

Newsweek, 81

Nicaragua, 114t

Nixon, Richard, 58

Non-Marxist socialism, 108

North Korea, 46–47

Nuclear power plants, 57

O

Obama, Barack, 68

Oil
arms purchases and, 71
British oil fields in Iran, 33
Israel and, 58

Khuzestan and, 26
modernization of Iran and, 57
shah and, 84, 86, 140
social effects of Iranian oil boom, 151
top oil-producing countries, 31t, 57, 66
United States interest in Iran and, 99
Olympics, 57
Opium trade, 68
Orientalism (Said), 91–92
Orwell, George, 97

P

Pahlavi, Mohammad Reza Shah
anti-shah movement, 12–16, *15*
assassination attempts, 59
book banning and, 89
cancer, 65, 70
Carter, Jimmy, and, 64
constitutional monarchy, 57
extradition demand, 44, 84
hereditary monarchy and, 6
Iranian response to Pahlavi's departure, 18–23, 139–140
Israel support, 5
land reforms, 5, 62, 124
liberal reform, 4–5, 51–53
Mossadegh, Mohammad, and, 125
photographs, *21*
regime collapse, 5–6, 12–13, 17–24, 26, 44–45, 123, 144
Shah Memorial, *27*
statues, 18, 22
US support of, 56–73
women's clothing restrictions and, 51–53
Pahlavi, Reza Shah, 51, 53, 100, 125
Pakistan, 173
Palestine Liberation Organization (PLO), 79–80

Palestinians, 61
Paraguay, 72
Paris (France)
hostage crisis and, 48
Khomeini, Ruhollah, exile, 5, 15, 62, 101–102, 138, 142
PBS (TV network), 78
Perloff, James, 56–68
Personal stories
British diplomat, 137–144
Iranian exiles, 172–177
Iranian professor, 145–156
Khomeini, Ruhollah, interview, 157–164
US embassy hostages, 165–171
Peru, 114t
Philippines, 72
Piettre, André, 57
Pirandello, Luigi, 49
Platypus Review (online magazine), 133–135
Postel, Danny, 129–135
Precht, Henry, 65
Price, David, 36
Price, Massoume, 100
Princeton University, 77
Prison, 59, *94*, 117, 119, 138, *147*, 174–175
Propaganda, 21–22
Prostitution, 118, 163–164

Q

Quandt, William, 91
Quran, 102, 119

R

Rabbi, Amir Hossein, 64–65

Race and Class (magazine), 92

Racism, 77

Rafsanjani, Akbar Hashemi, 126

Randal, Jonathan C., 17–24

Reagan, Ronald, 40

Rebel with a Cause (Behrooz), 130

Red Cross, 59

Reynolds, Frank, 75

Riots, 61–64, 125, *125*

Roberts, Allan, 36

Rockefeller, Nelson, 58

Roosevelt, Franklin D., 59

Royster, Vermont, 80

Russia, 31t, 127

S

Sadat, Anwar, 68, 95

Safavid dynasty, 12

Said, Edward W., 74–84, 89–90, 93–94

Saidzadeh, Mohsen, 119

Sanctions on Iran, 33, 40–41, 43, 45

Saudi Arabia, 20, 31t, 143

SAVAK (Iranian secret police), 12, 20, 23, 59–61, 70–71, 99, 150–151

Shah Memorial, *27*

Shah of Iran. *See* Pahlavi, Mohammad Reza Shah

Shaplen, Robert, 38–49

Shari'a law, 90, 100, 119

Shariati, Ali, 92, 107–108

Shariatmadari, Mohammad Kazem, 105, 140

Shia Islam
   explanation, 16n1
   imams and, 104, 105, 108, 142
   Islamic government and, 104

Khomeini, Ruhollah and, 4, 12, 62
   martyrdom and, 81, *82*, 85, 104, 108
   media and, 79
   political stance, 4
   Sunni Islam and, 26

Shirazi, Haeri, 118

Shoja'l, Zahra, 116

Shore, Peter, 35

Sickmann, Rocky, 165–171

Singh, Michael, 122–128

Souresrafil, Behrouz, 5

Soviet Union. *See* USSR

Spain, 100–102, 174

St. Louis Post-Dispatch, 75

Stone, I.F., 84

Stoning to death, 113, 115, 116

Strikes, 14–15

Sullivan, William, 65

Sullivan, Zohreh T., 172–177

Sunni Islam, 26, 104

Syria, 99

T

Taleghani, Azam, 54

Taleghani, Mahmoud, 54, 150, 158

Tariffs, 124

Tehran University, 20

Temple-Morris, Peter, 34

Temporary marriage, 118

Thailand, 177

Theocracy (Islamic Republic), 6, 25–28, 90, 116

Time (magazine), 81

Tobacco, 124

Today (TV program), 82

Turkamans, 26, 72

Turkey, 86
Turks, 72

U

Ulama (bazaar merchants), 13
United Nations, 33, 48
United Nations Convention on
  the Elimination of All Forms of
  Discrimination Against Women, 115
United Nations Special Rapportuer, 120
United States
    freeze of Iranian assets, 40–41
    "great satan," 46, 91
    Iraq war, 68, 78
    Islam and, 95
    oil production, 31t
    support of the shah, 56–68
    US embassy in Iran takeover, 6
    See also Hostage crisis of November
      1979; individual leaders
University of Illinois, 23
US Council on Foreign Relations (CFR),
  59, 63, 68
US Department of State, 120
US National Security Council (NSC), 42,
  58
USS Pueblo (ship), 46–47
USSR, 31t, 39, 58, 59, 66, 99, 132

V

Vance, Cyrus R., 39, 40, 42, 45
Velayat-e Faqeeh (Khomeini), 90–93
Velayat-e Faqeeh (supreme rule of mul-
  lahs), 5, 116, 120, 121
Vienna convention, 30, 32
Vietnam, 99
Violence against women, 114t, 116

Voice of America, 63
Voice of Israel, 63
Voting rights, 5, 113–114

W

Waldheim, Kurt, 48
Wall Street Journal, 75, 80
Walzer, Michael, 76, 91, 95
Washington Post, 79, 85, 91, 92
Western culture, 28, 141
White Revolution, 13
Women
    child custody and, 111, 118
    dress restrictions, 50–54, 111, *112*, 113,
      116–117
    employment restrictions, 117–118
    guards, *55*
    health care segregation, 118–119
    Inheritance rights, 113
    Iranian Green Revolution and, *131*
    Islamic Revolution and, 110–121
    Shari'a and, 119
    spousal violence and, 114t
    stoning to death and, 113, 115
    subordination, 95
    voting rights, 5, 113–114
    working conditions, 53, 115
World Court, 33
World War II, 63
World Was Going Our Way (Andrew and
  Mitrokhin), 5
Wyatt, Arthur, 30

Y

Yazdi, Mohammad, 111, 118
Yom Kippur War, 68
Yuenger, James, 81

Z

Zambia, 114t

Zanan (magazine), 120

Zarnett, David, 88–97

Zeins, Wally, 166

Zia-ul-Haq, Muhammad, 173

Zionists, 68, 161

Zoroastrianism, 100, 175